Table of Contents TOC

Introduction

Book Organization

Where possible, information is organized topically. Within topics, codes are arranged alphabetically. Exceptions occur where codes are used sequentially to perform specific tasks. In these cases, code explanations are organized in the order they are normally used. Where there are lists of index codes (i.e., hotpath listings and RES Star Information files) the order is alphabetical by topic.

Notations in This Book

Sabre code formats are highlighted with a bold font, i.e.: **HIDIR/HELP**. When shown like this, text must be entered ***exactly*** as it appears. Blanks, when required by the entry, are shown with the symbol ∧. When shown, the blank ***must*** be used. The Sabre network is ***not forgiving*** of format errors. Variable data, such as passcodes, flight numbers, etc., is enclosed in these brackets **<>**. The brackets are not found on any Sabre set, and should never be entered. Instead, they are replaced with the variable data as in the following example:
NS/<Flight #>/<Date>/<Departure Station> might be entered at a terminal with the characters: **NS/50/3/DFW**

Where applicable, examples are included with codes throughout this book in cases where they improve clarity. The general format used in the book is as follows:

CODE Description of the entry, followed by an **EXAMPLE**
CODEs are always at the start of the paragraph. **EXAMPLES** are always at the far right margin. Examples appear when the code includes variable data such as departure station or date.

The Sabre network uses various types of data in a variety of formats. The following definitions are used for variable data:

<Base> Crewmember's 3-letter coded bid status base.

<Date> Date, usually be abbreviated to the 1 or 2-digit day of the month only, i.e. **13** for the 13th of the current month. In general, Sabre goes to the closest 13th, which may be in the next month if the entry is made on the 30th day of the current month. If a specific format is required, this book specifies it with the **DDMMMYY** notation, i.e. **13MAY94**.

<Division> Division Code; Allowable codes are for domestic (**D**) and international (**I**)

<Equipment> Three-character fleet codes. Allowable codes are: **190 S80 320 330 737 757 767 777 787**

<Flight> Flight number

<Position> For pilots, see seat (below). For flight attendants, allowable codes are either the two digit position (**01**, **02**…) or are specified where different.

<Seat> Crewmember's current bid position (**CA**, **FO, FB**, and **FC**). **FB** & **FC** are not allowed on most entries.

<Station> 3-Letter code for departure/arrival station, as required. Where two stations are required, the arrival and departure stations are specified, i.e., **<Dep Station>/<Arr Station>**. Where not specified, i.e., **<Station>**, assume departure station.

<VAR> Variable data required for a code, defined in the descriptive paragraph; applies to that code only.

Special Codes Used in This Book

Online — Indicates a difference exists when using WebPC FOS to access the Sabre network from the Internet. This can be done from **www.aapilots.com** or **www.apfa.org**.

CP — Indicates the code applies only to cockpit crew members.

FA — Indicates the code applies only to flight attendants.

^ — Indicates a required space in a Sabre code format.

Code can only be printed, not displayed on screen

Code can only be displayed on screen, not printed

Note: *When needed for personal mode entries, codes are divided into flight attendant and pilot sections. Codes in these sections of chapter 3A and 3B are not designated with the* FA *and* CP *symbols. Index entries at the end of the book include these symbols.*

What This Book IS

This book is intended to provide a quick way to reference some of the most common Sabre® system entries. It includes entries available both from workplace or home computers. An attempt has been made to note exceptions—those entries which can only be made from Sabre system terminals, usually because the entry requires a dedicated printer, as opposed to those also available from other computers. This material is copyrighted--please don't photo-copy it.

What this Book IS NOT

The Computer Codes in this book are the exclusive property of **Sabre Inc.**, **American Airlines, Inc.** and the former **AMR Corporation**. This book is not officially sanctioned by those entities, however. The author offers for sale only the compilation and formatting of these codes, not the codes themselves. All codes have been tested by the author and worked at the time of publication (based on level of EPR). No guarantee written or implied is made as to the validity of the codes at the time of use, however. You must use this information carefully, practice, and look for the feedback given by the system to ensure the command you entered has resulted in the intended outcome. It is the intent of the author to provide information to make all of our jobs easier as well as more productive. This book is for general information purposes only. Current American Airlines and FAA procedures shall be used at all times. **AA®** Is a registered mark of **American Airlines**, **Inc**., and **Sabre** is a registered mark of an affiliate of **Sabre Inc.; IBM®**, **Raytheon®**, **ICOT®**, and **Tandy®** are all registered trademarks of their respective companies. **DIAL AA FLIGHT** is a service mark of **American Airlines, Inc**. ***Windows*** is a registered trademark of the **MicroSoft Corporation.**

Usage and Limitations

This book is produced as a reference tool for American Airlines personnel and the codes were last validated in 2017. At that time, every code was checked and worked properly. The author has now retired form American Airlines and makes no guarantee that codes herein are current or functional. They are provided as a reference and published as a service to those who still need to use the codes for official use in the performance of their work, during non-revenue travel and other authorized activities.

The codes documented in this book are the protected and owned by Sabre™, and the documentation of these codes was authorized by license agreement with Sabre, Inc. at the time of the agreement's activation.

1. General SABRE Information

Sabre Terminal Keyboards

Individual keys on the computer keyboard are listed with a round-edged border or with the character on the key as follows:

SABRE	Online	
ENTER	ENTER	Enter Key. Used to send codes to the Sabre network—shown in this book only when required more than once, and in specific order.
⊠	[	Change Key [Key substituted when Online. Usually shown in this book as ⊠.
▬	–	Name Key. Identifies the text following as a name. Usually shown in this book with the "–" symbol. Newer keyboard number pad "minus keys" work as well.
Σ	\	End Item Key. Separates data fields in some entries.
‡ or ¥	' (*Apostrophe*)	Cross of Lorraine Key. IBM and Tandy terminals use the ¥ symbol.

Keys having two functions execute the bottom function when pressed alone (clear the screen, in this case), and the top function (backspace left and delete the character to the left) when pressed *in combination with* the SHIFT key. Another common example is the PRINT + ENTER key. To enter codes, simply press the key. To enter the command and send the output to a printer, press the SHIFT key in combination with the PRINT + ENTER key

↵ BK SPACE CLEAR

Sabre Modes

The SABRE network has two modes of operation. **DECS** is used for flight and aircraft information, crew lists, bidding, etc. **RES** is used for passenger entries, such as flight listing, seating availability, and non-revenue-travel. Some terminals are used by either American Airlines or American Eagle. Before using a joint-use terminal, it must be in the correct mode i.e. American Airlines vs. American Eagle. To change modes, use the following entries:

//<Carrier Code> Enter/change airline mode. Allowable codes:
AA-American Airlines **MQ**-Envoy **TE**-regional partners
//AA, //MQ or **//TE**

Possible responses:

AA DECS .... *In DECS and signed in*
SIGN IN A-DECS .... *In DECS, but not signed in*
A. . . .AA .... *In RES and signed in*
SIGN IN A.................................... *In RES but not signed in*

⊠⊠DECS Change to DECS Mode
⊠⊠RES Change to RES Mode

Determining the Current Mode

To determine the current mode and sign in status of a terminal, use the following entries:

***M** Current mode (DECS/RES)
***S*P** Active agent & printer
‡J CRT Set address
‡T Tulsa time & date
S Active agent & set

Signing In—General

Before using a terminal, logging on to Sabre via PCFOS, you must tell the network ***who you are*** and ***verify your identity*** by use of your passcode. You tell the network ***who you are*** with your employee number. You ***verify that identity*** with your passcode. Your RES passcode must be changed every 45 days. DECS and PCFOS passcodes have no expiration, but should be changed periodically to ensure they remain secure. Change the code if you think someone may have observed your sign-in at a terminal which does not mask the data. The following codes accomplish sign-in functions:

DECS Sign-In Codes

//AA (Seldom required) Changes terminal partition from American Eagle DECS to American Airlines DECS

⊠⊠DECS Change Terminal from RES to DECS mode. Use **[[DECS** when online. Online

BSI<Employee#> ENTER **<Passcode>** Sign in to terminal and DECS only. "Times out" in about 5 minutes (DECS) or 3 minutes (DECS personal mode) if no entries are made. Time varies with employee category and terminal location; cannot be modified by users. **BSI123456** ENTER **MYCODE01**

HIP/<Employee#> ENTER **<Passcode>** Personal mode sign-in; times out if no entries are made for 3 minutes. You must first sign in to the terminal with a **BSI** sign-in to use this personal mode sign-in. **HIP/123456** ENTER **MYCODE01**

BSIP<Employee #>ENTER<Passcode> Simultaneously sign in to terminal, DECS, and personal mode.
BSIP123456 ENTER MYCODE01

HIX Signs the terminal out of your personal mode. Terminal remains signed in to DECS. Do this before leaving a terminal to protect your personal mode from changes made by the next user.

HIS/<Employee#> ENTER <Passcode> CP Initial sign in for a sequence. May only be done at your scheduled departure station.
HIS/234567 ENTER MYCODE01

HISS/<Employee#>/<Passcode> FA Sign in at airport for standby. **HISS/123456/MYCODE01**

HIDIR Enter Personal Mode Directory. Personal Mode must be entered first before HIDIR entry is allowed.

X ENTER Exit Personal Mode Directory (HIDIR)

***S*P** Display printer & agent (individual) signed in to terminal

BSO Basic agent Sign Out–Disconnects terminal from DECS until someone else signs in. Terminal remains in DECS mode. RES mode (if signed in) is still available and may be activated by changing to the RES mode (**☒☒RES**) until it times out.

DECS Sign In Error Messages

If signing in and you receive a **‡PASSCODE REQUIRED‡** message, you must sign-in by adding a slash and your passcode after the normal sign-in code. Examples of this entry follow. Your passcode ***will not be masked***, so use caution to protect its security. In addition, call FOS Control at ICS (817) 967-1848 for terminal reset.

BSI<Employee#>/<Passcode> Sign in to terminal and DECS only. Notes above apply. **BSI123456/MYCODE01**

HIP/<Employee#>/<Passcode> Enter personal mode, some terminals. **HIP/123456/MYCODE01**

RES Sign-In Codes

☒☒RES Change Terminal from DECS to RES mode. Use **[[RES** when online. Online

SI<EMPLOYEE #> ENTER <Passcode> ENTER RES mode sign in
SI123456 ENTER MYCODE01 ENTER

SO Sign Out–Disconnects terminal from RES. (Terminal stays in RES.) DECS (if signed in) is still available and may be activated by changing to the DECS mode (**☒☒DECS**) until it times out.

Passcode Rules & Help

These notes apply to Passcodes in DECS, RES, and PCFOS

For passcode changes–May be done by entering your current passcode, then using the TAB or ZOOM keys to reach the **NEW PASSCODE** field, then entering the new passcode. If you forget your passcode or need other assistance, contact FOS Control,

682-315-2367, email: DL_FOS@aa.com.

General Passcode Rules

- 8 Characters maximum, mixed numerals and alphabetical
- Cannot include Q or Z
- Cannot have 3 sequential letters ("AAA12345")
- Cannot be the same as either of the last two passcodes

Passcodes–DECS DECS Passcodes have no expiration

- Forgotten DECS/FOS or WSI Passcodes—FOS Control (24-7) **682-315-2367**

Passcodes–RES

- RES Passcodes must be changed every 45 days
- Forgotten RES passcodes—Contact your work supervisor
- WebPC/FOS Help Desk (general information, password change or dialup access tech support (M-F, 6:00AM to 2:00 PM, CST) **682-315-2367**. Use when at home.

General Access Issues

- Second Stage SABRE via Internet
- MobileFOS, Crew Checkin and WSI functionality
- IT Help Desk **480-693-6029**

Navigating the Sabre Screen

To move the cursor around the Sabre screen, simply use the arrow keys. For displays more than one screen long, a ‡, ¥ or ↕ symbol appears at the bottom right corner of the screen. To move among the pages, use the following entries. They allow you to negotiate through the screens, move to the top or bottom of the file, etc. In general, you remain in the display until you enter another command.

MDENTER View Next Screen (**M**ove or scroll **D**own)

MUENTER View Previous Screen (**M**ove or scroll **U**p)

MTENTER **M**ove to **T**op of Response

MBENTER **M**ove to **B**ottom (End) of Response

MD<Lines>ENTER View Next Screen (**M**ove or scroll **D**own). The **<Lines>** variable specified how many lines to scroll, or may be left blank as above. **MD5**

MD/<Search Text>ENTER RES only—Scrolls down until the specified text is found. *Example:* To search for a reference to "fares" in a Jetwire article specify the text **FARE**. **MD/FARE**

Re-Entering Text and Keyboard Shortcuts

Commands previously used may be easily re-entered without typing them again. An example might be an open time list which was displayed on screen, and which you decide you want to print. The following commands below allow you to do this without retyping the entire command.

Entering a command already on the screen: To do this, start by placing the cursor at the beginning of the command line by using the HOME key to get to the top line of the screen.

HOME Use this key to move the cursor to the top line of the screen or left position.

RESET Use this key to reset the cursor one line down, left screen edge.

→ Right arrow key—use to move across previously typed command text.

SHIFT + **END** Use these two keys in combination to move the cursor to the end of a line of text. Then, hitting the **ENTER** key will enter this line of text. Using **SHIFT** + **PRINT + ENTER** sends the results to a printer.

SHIFT + **↑**, or + **↓** Using this combination of keys scrolls up or down through previously entered commands and displays them on the current line. The cursor appears at the end of the line, and the command may be printed or reentered. Text may be edited by using the **→** and **←** keys, modifying text as needed. This feature helps when modifying repetitive entries such as **N3D** entry (open time, Domestic) by changing the **D** to an **I** to check International open time for the same date range. At some newer sets, the **ALT** or **CTRL** keys are used instead of the **SHIFT** key. These key strokes ***do not*** work on WebPC FOS Second Stage application, but ***do*** work on the WebPC FOS Full Screen application.

RE-ENT Re-Enter key. Used to re-enter the last command used. Helpful for repetitive entries, such as move down (**MD**) or next-in-list (**KQ**) commands.

Printer Commands

To designate a printer for your session, find the printer address. It is a six-character code, which is always on a label or written somewhere on the printer. The code usually contains both numbers and letters. Some terminals are set up so that one of the function keys designates the printer. This is usually the **F1** key when you are fortunate enough to have the terminal properly set up. To designate the printer manually, use the command: **PTR/<Printer Address>**, which might appear as: **PTR/1ABCDE**

If the printer is not responding, enter **RL/P** to release it. The reply should read: **RESTARTED/002 MSGS ON QUEUE**

If that does not work, or if you wish to stop a printer from printing a lengthy report, use the following commands, *in order*:

RL/<Printer Address>HOLD Print queue–**HOLD**. **RL/1ABCDEHOLD**

RL/<Printer Address>CLEAR Print queue–**CLEAR** incoming messages. **RL/1ABCDECLEAR**

RL/P Printer **R**e**L**ease & restart **P**rinter. **RL/P**

Other helpful printer-related commands include the following:

PTR/ Display a designated printer
PTR/END Undesignate a printer
***S*P** Display of designated printer and agent signed-in
RL/<Printer Address>STATUS Status of the designated printer **RL/1ABCDESTATUS**
DIR/HELP/CP/PTR or **DIR//FA/HELP/PTR** Printer help files

Sabre-Plus

Sabre-Plus is an interface that adds a layer of "user friendly" menus to The Sabre network. This interface, however, does not provide for crewmember operational entries, personal mode entries or general DECS use. Regular Sabre screen format is still available on the machine but you must toggle between Sabre-Plus and the basic Sabre mode.

To Toggle from Sabre-Plus to Basic Sabre Mode

CTRL **+ right** SHIFT keys–press simultaneously ***or***
ALT **+** S keys–press simultaneously

At this point, it will be necessary to change to DECS, sign in, initiate the printer, etc. If you have trouble finding the printer LNIATA symbolic address, call FOS Control at ICS **967-1848** for assistance. For information on signing in the printer, see page 11.

Note: *This is the only Sabre-Plus-related question crewmembers are supposed to be able to call FOS Control to ask, because crewmembers don't currently "require training in this mode." Go figure.*

To Toggle from Sabre to Sabre-Plus Mode

CTRL **+** ESC keys–press simultaneously ***or***
ALT **+** X keys–press simultaneously

Sabre Error Messages

General Error Messages

The Sabre network has a large number of possible error messages. Frequently, the errors result when a code is entered in the wrong Sabre mode. In other words, you entered the correct code, but the terminal was not in the mode you thought it was.

AGENT DISCONNECTED-INACTIVE OVER 15 MIN SIGN IN A This indicates the set has "timed out" and signed itself out of DECS or RES. ***Fix:*** Sign in again, then re-enter the code. **Note**: If you are in an Operations Area, the terminals should not sign out. If you get this message, simply enter the code again–it should work the second time.

FINISH ‡KET‡ OR IGNORE This commonly occurs when trying to sign out of DECS while in a queued list such as a maintenance KVA entry. ***Fix:*** To sign out, type **KIG** ENTER, **KQVR** ENTER, and **BSO** ENTER. You will need to sign in to make further entries.

FINISH OR IGNORE This most commonly occurs in RES, when working with a PNR or other scripted area. ***Fix:*** Type **I** ENTER

[Ignore]. (Do not enter **ET** ENTER unless you are working with a PNR and intend to save changes you made.)

‡FORMAT‡ Your entry format is incorrect. The Sabre network may "recognize" part of it but has no suggestions. An example of a format error response indicating Sabre is able to recognize part of the entry and suggests the proper format is **‡FLT/DT/STA‡** *Fix:* Recheck the format and re-enter.

***INVALID ACTION CODE** The computer doesn't recognize the entry. *Fix:* Use **//AA** entry, and check to see whether you are in DECS or RES, as in the preceding entry.

‡INVALID ENTRY‡ or **‡INVALID KEY‡** Several possibilities:

- Someone left the terminal in the HIDIR (personal mode directory.) *Fix:* Type **X** ENTER. If you get message "**YOU HAVE EXITED THE FOS DIRECTORY**," the problem is solved.
- Someone left the terminal with an open PNR (Passenger Name Record, discussed in the RES chapter.) or BMAS file (used by the baggage system operators). Both of these are sub-modes of RES or TIMS. *Fix:* The following entries should solve the problem: **IG** ENTER **SO** ENTER **⊠⊠DECS** ENTER
- Terminal was in Eagle mode. (**‡INVALID KEY‡** message generally results from this) *Fix:* Type **//AA** ENTER.
- If none of these methods work, something is probably broken and may be beyond your ability to troubleshoot. *Fix:* Call FOS/Hardware Control (see below) to help you reset the terminal, or use another terminal.

‡INVALID FORMAT‡ If you are sure the format you used was correct, you were probably in the wrong mode. *Fix:* Type **⊠⊠DECS** or **⊠⊠RES** as appropriate.

INVLD ACT CODE Conversational mode session ended. May indicate FOS Directory time-out has occurred. *Fix:* Re-enter personal mode and FOS directory.

‡NO CARR/RTN ON LINE <#>‡ During a personal mode **HI0** (**HI**-zero) entry you didn't hit RETURN before the text wrapped at the end of a line. **<#>** Indicates which line was too long. *Fix:* Use the arrow keys to place the cursor at the end of the line in question and hit the RETURN key. Then use the arrow keys to move back to the end of your message.

SECURITY RESTRICTION Indicates you are making an entry not authorized for your EPR. If this is entry you can normally make, such as placing yourself on the makeup list.. This would occur if someone else signed the terminal in.
Fix:, sign out and sign in again. Then retry the entry.

Phone Numbers for Error Reporting and Assistance

Forgotten Passcodes– For DECS/FOS or WSI passwords, call FOS control-ICS **(682)-315-2367**.For forgotten RES passwords, see your supervisor, or contact EDS security at SEASystemsSecurity@eds.com

1 SABRE - General

For any of the following errors, call the American Airlines IT Help desk at **(918)-833-3434** or **(918)-833-3333**

Hardware Problem–If you are having a hardware problem, such as a broken printer, etc.,

Software Problem–If you are having what appears to be a software problem with a RES entry,

‡CALL TCC ASAP‡ Report the entry/entries which resulted in this error message. Also call for terminal-related problems.

‡ERR CALL FOR ASSISTANCE‡ Use the entry, //RETURN to obtain terminal information

2. General DECS Codes

DECS is used for operational and personal mode information access. For Crewmembers' Personal Mode, see Chapter 3, page 29.

Crew Listings & Information

NS/<Flight> Flight crew listing, aircraft and gates, for either the current or next leg with that flight number. **NS/333**

NS/<Flight#>/<Date>/<Station> Flight crew listing, aircraft, gates **NS/333** for today, or **NS/333/13SEP/DFW**

NSD/<Flight#>/<Date>/<Station> Flight crew listing, deadheading crewmembers **NSD/333** for today, or **NSD/333/13SEP/DFW**

NSO/<Flight#>/<Date>/<Station> Operating flight crew listing, no deadheaders **NSO/333** for today, or **NSO/333/13SEP/DFW**

NSG/<Flight#>/<Date>/<Station> Flight crew listing with crew origination information **NSG/333** for today, or **NSG/333/13SEP/DFW**

NST/<Flight#>/<Date>/<Station> Flight crew listing, with nicknames **NST/333/13SEP/DFW**

Sequence and Schedule Information

HFS/<Position>/<Flight#>/<Date>/<Dep Station> Display sequence containing specified flight **HFS/FB/333/13/ORD**

HSS/<Position>/<Sequence>/<Date> Sequence Details **HSS/FO/3101/13** *or* **HSS/FO/3101/13MAY**

21/<EMP> Bid Result by Employee Number **21/234567**

22P/<Month>/<Selection>/<Base> Bid selection as originally scheduled, and who held it **22P/OCT/1396/DFW**

26A<Airline Code>/<Dep Station>/<Arr Station>/<Date> Flights scheduled non-stop between stations. Airline codes:

MQ Envoy **TE** Regional Partners
Blank Legacy AA Mainline **26AMQ/DFW/PHX/13** or **26A/DFW/PHX/13**

26K<Airline Code>/<Dep Station>/<Arr Station>/<Date>
Connecting flights between stations. (Includes some connections RES and NTRP may not list.) Airline codes may be added as in **26A** above. **26K/ORD/SEA/13** or **26KMQ/CLT/RDU/13**

26B<Airline Code>/<Dep Station>/<Arr Station>/<Date>
Direct ***and*** connecting flights between stations. Airline codes as above. **26B/BNA/ORD/13** or **26BMQ/LGA/ORD/13**

Note: *Trip trades codes detailed beginning on page 26, with pilots' specific information starting on page 35, and for flight attendants on page 38.*

Flight Plan-Related Displays And Codes

Important Note: Do not experiment with these codes. Entries should be made ***only for your own flight as necessary***. Some generate closeout data for current flights, so errors can cause confusion.

IB*<EAST or **WEST>** Track message summary **IB*EAST**

SLS*<EAST or **WEST> /NO** Track message, detailed **SLS*EAST/NO** or **SLS*WEST/NO**

IZ*ALL/<Dep Station>/<Arr Station>/<Optional Variable>
Flight plan route options. In place of **ALL**, use **S** (ATC Routes), or **C** (Company Routes). **<Optional Variable>** uses **ATC** to show ARTC text only, or route number for specific route. **IZ*ALL/ORD/BNA** or **IZ*C/ORD/BNA/ATC**

IFC/<PT 1>/<PT 2> Distance & bearing between two navigation points **IFC/RZC/FSM** or **IFC/ARINA/DFW**

IFC/A/<Station 1>/A/<Station 2> Great circle and rhumb line distance and bearing between airports **IFC/A/ORD/A/GRR**
May use 4-letter ICAO identifiers **IFC/A/KORD/A/EGLL**

IK*<Waypoint> Look up latitude and longitude for specified navigation waypoint **IK*BAMBI**

JP*<Flight#>/<Date>∧<Station> Print flight plan, weather and appended messages. Space is ***required*** between **<Date>** and **<Departure Station>**. (***only***) **JP*333/27∧ORD**

JPY<Flight#>/<Date DD>∧<Departure Station>∧AGREE
Electronically sign flight plan **JPY333/27∧ORD∧AGREE**

JPY*<Flight#>/<Date DD>∧<Departure Station> Verify status of electronically signed flight plan **JPY*333/27∧ORD**

ACARS Signing of Flight Plan

MD-80, 767 Basic .... **Misc <21>** ENTER
.... **<Six Digit Employee Number>** ENTER
.... **<Last 4 Digits of PIC License Number>** ENTER
TWA MD-80 .... **Misc <21>** ENTER
.... **<Six Digit Emp No. + License Last 4>** ENTER
757 .... **Misc <22>** ENTER
.... **<Six Digit Emp No. + License Last 4>** ENTER
737, 767 Pegasus .... **Free Text Message**
.... **<Six Digit Emp No. +License Last 4>** ENTER
320, ACARS Entry, Preflight page, access with L or R arrow key . **<Six Digit Emp No.>**, **<License Last 4>** ENTER

JPD<Flight#>/<Date>∧<Departure Station> Flight plan, *no* appended messages or load plan. (*or*) **JPD333/27∧ORD**

JPE<Flight#>/<Date>∧<Departure Station> Flight plan summary with fuels (*only*) **JPE333/27∧ORD**

JPF<Flight#>/<Date>∧<Departure Station> Flight plan summary, ATC-filed routing only. (*or*) **JPF333/27∧ORD**

JPR<Flight#>/<Date>∧<Departure Station> Flight plan and appended messages only; no weather, TPS or F/A briefing. May be viewed on screen or printed. (*only*) **JPR333/27∧ORD**

JPX<Flight#>/<Date>∧<Station> Print flight attendant briefing information. (*or*) **JPX333/27∧ORD**

JS*<Station> Station geographic coordinates. Adding **/ADR** displays data addresses. **<Station>** May be either 3-letter station or 4-letter ICAO code. Both codes are in the response, so it can be used to decode a known identifier. Examples—London, Heathrow. **JS*LHR** or **JS*EGLL** or **JS*LHR/ADR**

TP*/<Station>/<Flight#>/<Ship#>/<Flaps>/<PTOW>/<Runways> Print runway departure plan. **PTOW** Entry is in hundreds of pounds, i.e. 125,431 pounds would be entered **"1254"** **TP*/DFW/333/135/10/1254/17L,17R**

VAT/<Station> Runway takeoff surface length, and intersection takeoff data used for **TP***, **VAA**, and **VAA** entries. **VAT/DEN**

RF8000∧ENG Airport temporary analysis codes & formats.

XEP/<Flight#>/<Date>/<Dep Station> Connecting passenger information & sources **XEP/333/13SEP/DFW**

XPZ<Station> Exact station Zulu and local time. If **<Station>** is left blank, Zulu and local time at HDQ. **XPZ** or **XPZLHR**

Load-Related Entries

Important Note: Do not experiment with these codes. Entries should be made ***only concerning your own flight***, and only ***as necessary***. Some generate a new closeout for an actual flight and could cause a flight to take off with erroneous takeoff data.

WBDF<Flight#>/<Date>∧<Station> Print load plan/TPS (*only*) **WBDF333/27SEP∧ORD**

WBD*<Flight#>/<Date>∧<Station> Load plan/TPS (Same as **WBDF**, but *or* allowed) **WBD*333/27SEP∧ORD**

WBS*<Flight#>/<Date>∧<Station> Display passenger count on which the load plan is based **WBS*333/27SEP∧DFW**

WBP*<Flight#>/<Date>∧<Station> Display load planing passenger ***and*** baggage data. **WBP*333/27SEP∧DFW**

Weather-Related Entries

General Weather Information

RW*/<Station> Display runway wind components **RW*/ORD**

RW*/<Station>/<Runway> Runway wind component **RW*/COS/17L**

RW*/<Station>/<Runway>/<Direction>/<Velocity> Wind component for specified conditions. **RW*/COS/17L/200/17**

SLT*<Station> Display station weather and 10 alternates **SLT*CLT**

SLT*<Station>/<SA or **TAF>** Display station weather, specifying either **SA** (surface observations), or **TAF** (ICAO format surface observations.) **SLT*GHR/SA**

Optionally, add **/ALL** to include forecast **SLT*GHR/TAF/ALL**

SLS*<Station> Display current weather **SLS*ORD**

SLS*<MIA or **SFO>/WH** Hurricane forecasts; **MIA**–Atlantic, **SFO**–Pacific **SLS*MIA/WH**

SLA*<CA or **TS>/ALL** Clear air (**CA**) or thunderstorm (**TS**) reports. **SLA*CA/ALL**

SLS*MK<1, **2** or **3>/WS1** Convective weather SIGMETs for East (**1**), Central (**2**), or Western (**3**) US. **SLS*MK2/WS1**

SLS*<Station>/<Type> Weather, current and forecast, plus a Field Report. Options for **<Type>** include:

National Weather Service Forecast		General Information	
AFC	Clouds & upper level WX**	**FC**	Field report*
WS	NWS station reports.**	**NO**	NOTAMS*
WAS	AIRMET Reports.**	**UA1**	Pilot reports*
AFT	Turbulence and LLWS	**ALL**	* Items above & TAF

SLS*ORD/FC or **SLS*BOS/WS**

Available only for **BOS, **CHI**, **DFW**, **MIA**, **SLC**, **SFO**, **HNL**. For a current SIGMET, add the first letter. In **BOS** example above, **J** displays current SIGMET Juliet 1. **SLS*BOS/WSJ**

Other SL Entry Options:

SLTD<Station> .Station observation and changeover altimeter setting **Note**: *This is the most recent in the system, and could be inaccurate.* **SLTDORD**

SLTF<Station> Current weather in clear-text format (No abbreviations; similar to that on F/A Briefing.) **SLTFORD**

SLWA<Station> Surface reports for last 24 hours, Abbreviated format **SLWADFW**

SLWZ<Station> Surface reports for last 24 hours, full report (not abbreviated as in **SLWA** above) **SLWZDFW**

SLWB<Flight#>/<Date—DD>∧<Dep Station> Print flight plan release weather briefing **SLWB333/27∧DFW**

SLWR<Flight>/<Date—DD>∧<Dep Station> Print flight plan weather brief information **SLWR333/13∧ORD**

Regional Weather Reports

SLGA Listing of region names

SLGD<REGION> List stations in specified region **SLGDSPAIN**

SLG*<Region>/<Type> Regional weather . Options for **<Type>** are **NO** or **UA1.** See **SLS*** entry above. **SLG*EUROPE/UA1**

Internet Weather Resources

Pilots have access to Internet weather information through WSI's web site. The address is **http://www.pilotbrief.com**

Initial sign on user name is **AA<employee #>.** **AA123456**

Initial passcode is lower case "American" **american**

Weather Help Files

DIR/FLT/INTL/TAF Abbreviation codes for Meteorological Reports (METARs) & Terminal Area Forecasts (TAFs).

DIR/FLT/WEA Directory of weather entry formats

Note: *Not all listed codes in this index work.*

RF8000Q∧TMP Celsius/Fahrenheit conversion chart

Airport Analysis & TAA Entries

AWT/<Station>/<TAA #> Display temporary airport analysis **AWT/DEN/94–13**

VAX/ALL/<A, I, or **T>** Lists all Active or Inactive TAAs with a short description of each. Using **T** lists effective dates and **T**imes for both active and inactive TAAs. **VAX/ALL/T**

VAX/<Station>/T Same as above, for specified **<Station>**, including effective times. **VAX/RDU/T**

VAX/<Station> Airport Analysis Runway Data–Number of files stored, by equipment codes and aircraft specifications. (*Not* ***temporary*** airport analysis.) **VAX/DEN**

Flight Status and Tracking

FI<Flight#>/<Date>∧<Dep Station> Display flight status ***projected*** times (GMT) and fuels at flight plan points; ***actual*** times for changeover & position reports. **FI333/27∧DFW**

FIL∧<Flight#>/ Status of inbound flight **FIL∧333/**

FIL∧<Flight#>/<Date>∧<Dep Station>∧APAX Flight status summary **FIL∧333/13SEP∧DFW∧APAX**

FIL<Flight#>/<Date>∧<Dep Station> Display flight status, local times, no Flight Plan points. **FIL333/27∧DFW**

FIL<Flight#>/<Date>∧LEGS Display flight status summary. **FIL333/27∧LEGS**

DY* Displays a complete list of possible delay codes.

DY*<Code Number> Delay code definition **DY*60**

FL∧<Flight#>/<Date>∧<Dep Station>∧<Variable> Displays various categories of information concerning a specific flight. Possibilities **<Variables>** are as follows:

AA... Dispatcher changes
DC... Diversion
DM... Delays assigned to flight
FF... Miscellaneous
GG... Gate messages
JR... Flight plan release
PR... ACARS Messages ...
RD... Stub ....
RN... Aircraft change..........
WB... Load related...............
WX... Weather related ....
XL... Cancellation ....

To print all of the above information with a single entry (as well as other additional information), leave the variable blank, and press SHIFT + ENTER

FL∧333/13SEP∧DFW∧DM or **FL∧333/13SEP∧DFW**

Hotel Information

DIR/HTL/<1st Letter of City>/<Station> Regular layover hotel & station information. Example is for **Q**uito, Ecuador which has station code **UIO** **DIR/HTL/Q/UIO**

DIR/HTL/VMC/ALL Hotel information; FA variable manning

DIR/HTL/HELP Hotel formats & examples.

HIHTL/<Flight #>/<Date DD>/<Origination Station> Hotel information & voucher printout. Available for last flight of sequence duty day. Asterisk [*] next to crewmember name indicates voucher required. Includes relocation information if applicable. **HIHTL/333/13/DFW**

Station Phone Numbers

DIR/FLT/FONE/BASE/<Base> Chief pilot, flight administration, etc. **DIR/FLT/FONE/BASE/ORD**

DIR/FLT/FONE Phone number help file information

RF7700 FONE Flight Department phone number index

RF5432<A through ?>∧<Station> Station phone and other information. Stations have varying numbers of files, **A** through whatever is needed. **RF5432F∧DFW**

Hub Complex and Gate Information

At hub stations, current complex information can be accessed with several commands. These are helpful when trying to determine if a complex is behind due to weather, etc.

GILDISW∧A∧<A or **D>∧<Station>∧<Time>–<Time>∧<Date DDMMM>** All flights arriving during time block specified. The display format is similar to the information screens in the terminal. **<A** or **D>** is for **A**rriving or **D**eparting flights

GILDISW∧A∧D∧DFW∧0945–1345∧13OCT

The first **A** in the code is the portion of the complex to be examined, (**A**ll) and may be replaced with **N**orth, **S**outh, **E**ast or **W**est. **GILDISW∧W∧D∧DFW∧0945–1345∧13OCT**

RGG∧<Station>∧<Equipment>∧<Date DDMMM>∧<Time>∧<Time> Flights in and out of specified station in specific time period. **ALL** May be used in place of equipment code to display all affected aircraft **RGG∧DFW∧320∧13OCT∧0945∧1345**

PI*<Flight>/<Date>∧<Dep Station> Passengers connecting gate information for a given flight **PI*1611/11OCT∧DFW**

DT<D or **A>∧<Station>∧A∧<Time>/<Time>∧<Date DD>** Gate plan, **A**rriving or **D**eparting flights. Replacing **A** between station and time with **G<Gate>** shows departures and arrivals for that gate; not updated at all stations. **DTD∧DFW∧A∧1500/1545∧11** or **DTA∧ORD∧GK6A∧1200/2000∧13**

RGT<Station>/<Gate>∧<Time>/<Time> Planned gate activity. The **<Time>** variables are optional. **RGTORD/K6A** or **RGTORD/K6A∧1300/1500**

Maintenance and Logbook Entries

Maintenance Status and Actions

KLA*<Aircraft#> Display last maintenance entry **KLA*2AA**

KVA/<Aircraft#>/ALL/ALL/OPEN Open maintenance items for a specific aircraft **KVA/251/ALL/ALL/OPEN**

KVA/<SHIP#> Display aircraft maintenance log **KVA/452**

KVA<# Days>/<Aircraft#>/<System #> Aircraft maintenance history for a specific system. Allowable system codes are listed in file **RF8000∧ATA** **KVA3/2AA/61**

KVA<# Days>/<Aircraft#>/ALL Maintenance items for aircraft, for **<# DAYS>**. If **<# DAYS>** is left blank, one day is assumed. **KVA3/251/ALL** or **KVA/251/ALL**

Adding **<System Code>** results in data as **KVA** entry above for a specific system. (For possible system codes, see **RF8000∧ATA**.) **KVA3/251/ALL/30**

Adding **/P** displays only numbered items; maintenance inspections included without **/P** suffix. **KVA3/251/ALL/P**

KQ or **KQR** Maintenance or other items, show next in sequence.

KQVR Review completed before end of list (*Optional*)

RGL<Station> Display inbound flight open items **RGLGRR**

RF5903∧SYS FMR Codes

RF7700∧EQP Maintenance code summary

Systems-Specific Information

JCA*<Aircraft#> Aircraft engine history. **JCA*851**

JCE*<Aircraft#>/<Engine#>/T Recorded engine parameters at T/O. Engine number is by installed position, i.e., **1** or **2**. Delete **/T** suffix for cruise. **JCE*218/2/T** or **JCE*218/2**

JDM*<Aircraft#> Display aircraft data record **JDM*2CA**

JV*<Aircraft#> Aircraft restriction summary **JV*2AB**

RGEY/<Equipment> Listing of aircraft having the specified system installed. Allowable system codes are found in the table for each aircraft, **JDM*** entry above. **RGEY/ACARS**

MEL & SEL Codes

SGL<AIRCRAFT#> Display aircraft SEL **SGL2AA**
RGMN<Aircraft#> MEL items for specific aircraft **RGMN251**

Aircraft Schedules & Fleet Information

Aircraft Schedule Information

RF∧10∧SEC Listing of flights having cleared customs
RGG<Station>/<Equipment>/<DDMMM> Routing for all aircraft of specified equipment type through **<STATION>**. Includes passenger connection info. **RGGMEM/320/13OCT**
RGA<Aircraft#>/<Y or **F** *Optional*>**<Days** *Optional*> Aircraft origin & routing; Without suffix, shows only current day's schedule. **/Y** Shows one day before and after today. **/F** Shows specified days forward, or one if days left blank. **RGA251/F2**
RGS<Station> Aircraft routing through a station **RGSOKC**
RGN<Aircraft#> Routing for a particular aircraft. **RGN851**

Information by Fleet

JD*<Aircraft#> A/C weight and systems specifications **JD*2CA**
JD*ALL Specifications for fleet aircraft
JE*RLS Daily status report summary
JQ*ALL Total number of aircraft currently in each fleet with two-digit codes for each sub-fleet.
RE*<Equipment> Seating information by aircraft type **RE*757**
RES AA aircraft fleet total
RGF<Equipment> Real-time fleet status **RGF320**
RGK/<Equipment> Broken airplane listing by type **RGK/777**
RGU/<Equipment> Unassigned aircraft, by fleet. **ALL** may be substituted for fleet type. **RGU/777**
RF8<Equipment>∧NNN Ship numbers for aircraft in a specified fleet **RF8757∧NNN**

Indexed Information

RF5002∧DEC Flight Plan help screen
RF5300∧PC PC-FOS Information
RF5903∧SYS FMR Codes
RF5400A∧MOD Previous day ops summary. **RF5400A∧MOD**
RF5432<A through G>∧<Station> Station Information–phones, door codes, etc. Most stations have one file. Larger stations also a "**B**" file, and others if necessary. **RF5432C∧DFW**
RF7700<Variable>∧MAN Current manual revisions for various fleets. If the **<Variable>** is left out, an index of panels for all of the aircraft fleets is displayed. See next page for description of allowable variables. **RF7700B∧MAN**

- **A:** FM Part I, US High Charts, MEL General
- **B:** FM Pt. II

RF7700∧<Fleet> Fleet manual revisions, specified fleet. Allowable abbreviations: **DC9**, **B777**, **B737** or **757/767**. (**A320** not active.) **RF7700∧DC9**
RF7700∧HELP Index of Reference Files (RF) for crewmembers
RF7700∧<Variable> Various information displays including:

BID	Bids, standing	**KEY**	Common codes &

CREW	Crew-related information		abbreviations
DATA	Personal data update	**MAN**	Manual revisions
EQP	Aircraft related codes	**PERS**	Personal Mode
FONE	Phone number codes	**RLS**	Flight Planning

RF7700∧BID or **RF7700∧RLS**

RF7700∧IAB Immediate Attention Bulletins
RF7700∧KEY Index of RF file key words & abbreviations
RF8001∧ACAR Active ACARS stations **RF8001 ACAR**
RF8000∧TOA Takeoff alternate distances. For information only. Part 1 information is kept current and supersedes this listing.

<u>NOTE</u>: *A summary of HIDIR directories is found in Appendix 1.*

PER

3. DECS Personal Mode– Flight Crews

Personal Mode Sign-In

Personal mode sign-in procedures are below. For a complete discussion of sign-in procedures, see Chapter 1, General Sabre Information, pages 8-10. For explanation of the codes used in this book (i.e., **< >**, ʌ, , etc.), see page 4.

HIP/<Employee#> ENTER **<Passcode>** Enter personal mode
HIP/123456 ENTER **MYCODE01** ENTER

HIP/<Employee#>/<Passcode> Personal mode entry, some terminals (see page 9). **HIP/123456/MYCODE01**

HIS/<Employee#> ENTER **<Passcode>** Sign in for sequence. Also confirms fit for duty on first flight of the sequence.
HIS/123456 ENTER **MYCODE01** ENTER

HIFIT/<Flight#>/<Date>/<Station>/<Dep Time *Optional*>
CP Certify Fit for Duty for next leg of sequence. Use departure time for duplicate flight number if needed.
HIFIT/64/DFW or **HIFIT/64/DFW/1055**

HIS/<Employee#>!<Passcode> Sign In Format—PCFOS and Raytheon terminals. ENTER **HIS/123456!MYCODE01**

HISS/<Employee#>/<Passcode> FA Sign in at airport for standby **HISS/123456/MYCODE01**

HIX Exit Personal Mod

HIDIR-Personal Mode Directory

The HIDIR Mode is filled with useful information, but it is not user friendly. In order to access any code in DECS with the prefix "**HI**," the a user must be signed in to personal mode. This includes the HIDIR Mode.

After signing in to personal mode, you can access the HIDIR main menu by typing **HIDIR** and pressing ENTER. From that point until exiting HIDIR, ***no DECS code entries are available***. Two other options are available. The first is to use numbers displayed on each panel to select menu items. The second is to use the ***hotpath shortcuts*** shown to for each menu item. From any page within the HIDIR area, typing **DIR** plus the rest of the shortcut takes you to the desired screen. From outside HIDIR, in DECS, the entry would be **HIDIR** plus the codes for the panel desired. An example would be **HIDIR/HELP/FA/HI–** for a complete list of flight attendant personal mode entries. This entry goes from DECS directly into HIDIR and to the desired menu item. Had you already been in the HIDIR mode, the entry would be shortened to **DIR/HELP/FA/HI–**. For cockpit crewmembers, these entries would be **HIDIR/HELP/CP** from DECS, and **DIR/HELP/CP** from within the HIDIR directory. In either case, before accessing a DECS command, the **X** command to exit HIDIR is needed. A list of some of the most common HIDIR directory hotpaths is found at Appendix 1.

Monthly Bidding Entries

No attempt is made here to completely describe the bidding process. ***Most of this section is obsolete due to PBS bidding***. To access the instructions and print them out, use the following commands: **HIDIR/HELP/CP/BID** CP, or **HIDIR/FA/BID/HIB** FA ENTER

A screen will appear with several bidding-related topics. To print instructions on each of the topics (or any one) select the number corresponding to the topic desired, and press ENTER. When the first screen comes up, Print the Text with the command **PT** ENTER. You may access any of the help menus directly any time you are in HIDIR mode by typing **HIDIR/ HELP/CP/BID/<Menu Item>**, i.e., **MENU**, **HIBI**, etc.

```
HIB BIDDING INFORMATION
------------------------------------------------------------
 SELECT ITEM NUMBER DESIRED THEN DEPRESS ENTER
------------------------------------------------------------
1 HIB BIDDING INFORMATION                          / HIB /
2 HIB BIDDING - EXAMPLE OF MAIN MENU              / MENU /
3 HIB BIDDING ABBREVIATED INSTRUCTIONS            / HIBI /
4 BID STATUS ENTRIES                              / STAT /
5 BID ASSOCIATED ENTRIES                           / ENT /
```

Other monthly bid-related commands are as follows:

HIB Bid Ballot Mode entry
HIB/* Bid Ballot Display
RF7700ΛBID Bidding Initial Help Screen (Monthly)
HIDIR/HELP/CP/BID/HIB Help menu for HIB mode. CP
HIDIR/FA/BID/HELP Help Menu Display for HIB Mode. FA
HIBM Action Menu Display for Bidding FA
HIMAX Individual monthly maximum time legal for individual pilot.
3T*/C/<Base> Relief lines for current month FA **3T*/C/DFW**

3 Personal Mode

Vacation Bidding

Vacation bank and history may be accessed at any time in DECS personal mode by entering **HIVCBANK**

Instructions for use of vacation bank can be found at the HIDIR shortcut **HIDIR/CNTC/VAC/VBNK**.

Vacation bidding panels may be accessed during the bid-proffer for vacation bidding with the following entries:

HIVC Vacation Bidding System Entry
HIVC/* Display Vacation Bid

Bidding for pilots is accomplished through the AA Pilots web site, www.aapilots.com, **AA Scheduling/Vacation Bidding**.

Trip Trades

Trip trades, pickups, drops, and postings can be accomplished with the codes in this section. Information is organized below into 1) finding a trip you want, and 2) picking that trip up in a trade or other transaction. Much of may be superseded by the Trip Trade System (TTS) and Preferential Bid System (PBS) functions. As of this writing, however, all of these commands still work for manual entry of trades.

Finding Sequences for Trip Trades or Pickup

Trip trades may be accomplished easily. The difficult step is to find a trip. For flight attendants the Trip-Trading Bulletin Board is the easiest source, accessed by the command **HIBOARD**. It is fairly user-friendly and may be used to find trips either to drop or pick up.

For pilots, there is a general trip trade help screen which displays formats for most common codes. It is:

HITRIP Trip trade commonly used entry formats

Other codes (some displayed in HITRIP) are as follows:

HIFIND/<Day> Show legal open trips. Displays sequence number only, unlike an N4 entry which shows much more (*see below*.) Displays sequences in or out of the user's division—shows domestic sequences even if user is international. **HIFIND/13**
Adding **DFP** to the end including those which require changing of duty free periods. Sequences which ***require*** DFP adjustment each have an asterisk (*) **HIFIND/13/DFP**

__Note__: *You need not be in personal mode to access open time entries. There are some differences between pilot and flight attendant open time entries. For that reason, pilot entries are grouped in the* **Personal Mode—Pilots** *section on page 33, and F/A open time codes are in the* **Personal Mode—Flight Attendants** *section on page 38.*

Trading, Posting, or Picking Up a Trip

Once you have found a trip in open time or held by another crewmember willing to trade, use the following entries to complete the transaction. First, verify you and the other person have authorized trip trading. The following entries are related to this:

HIY Set trip trade authorization. View **HI7** to verify status. When status is **YES**, *no TT entry appears* on **HI1** top line.

HIN Unset trip trade authorization. **HI1** verifies. With status **NO**, **HI7** *has no TT entry*, but **HI1** top line reads **TT–NO**.

Posting or Deleting a Trip for Pickup

HIPOST/<Sequence #>/<Date>/<Pay Option> Post a trip to open time. A trip posted to open time ***is still the posting crew-member's responsibility*** *until it is picked up*. E-6 Message confirms a trip has been picked up from the posted list. Pay options are **PVD** or **CPA** for credited drop, or **UNC** for uncredited drop. Add **/D** to delete a posting. **HIY** ***not*** required.

HIPOST/123/13SEP/PVD or **HIPOST/123/13SEP/D**

PER

Trip Trade Test Mode

Trip Trade functionality includes a practice mode. When learning how to trade, it is advisable to practice with the ***Trip Trade Test Mode***. The following steps are used to enter test mode:

HIP/<Employee#> Enter personal mode if not there. See p. 8

HTT/<Your Employee#>/<Other Employee#> Enter Trip Trade Test Mode; you are **A**, other is **B** **HTT/12345/54321**

For a trip in open time, substitute **OPEN** for the second employee number. **HTT/123456/OPEN**

After test mode entry, all codes are the same as live trip trades.

Actual Trip Trade Mode

In active mode, the changes you tested will actually take effect. So be careful! The following commands are used.

HT/<1ST Employee #>/<2nd Employee #> Enter trip trade mode. Entering **HT** alone specifies open time in place of the 2nd Employee. In either case, **A** specifies the sequence you are ***giving up***, and **B** represents the sequence you are ***gaining***, and that **B** (crewmember or open time list) is ***giving up***. Examples:

Trade with another crewmember: **HT/123456/654321**

Response
```
A-123456 SMITH RJ
B-654321 JONES JR
```

Trade with open time: **HT**

Response
```
A-123456 SMITH RJ
B-OPEN SEQ LIST
```

Two prefixes are used for trading sequences—**HTS** for **T**rading **S**equences, or **HTO** for **T**rading **O**ne-way, either dropping to a pilot or open time, ***or*** picking up from open time but no trip drop or trade.

HTS/A/<Sequence>/<Date> Sequence crewmember **A** is trading ***away*** **HTS/A/123/13SEP**

HTS/B/<Sequence>/<Date>/<Seat> Sequence crewmember **B** is trading ***away*** **HTS/B/321/13SEP/FB**

HTO/A/<Sequence #>/<Date>/<Pay Option> Drop trip into open time. Pay options are **PVD** or **CPA** for credited drop, or **UNC** for uncredited drop. CP **HTO/A/123/13SEP/CPA**

HTO/B/<Sequence #>/<Date>/<Position> Pick up trip from open time or posted sequence list. Allowable positions are **CA**, **FO**, **FB**, **FC**, or **FE**. CP **HTO/B/123/13SEP/FB**

HTO/<A or B>/<Sequence>/<Date> Optional Exchange Entries: use HTO instead of HTS FA **HTO/A/3101/13SEP**

HTMD Move duty-free periods

HZ Complete transaction. If you entered the incorrect sequence or date you will have 3 chances for corrections. If the transaction is complete, an E-6 is sent to the other crewmember.

Trip Trade Example—Trading with another crewmember:

Enter trip trade mode **HT/123456/654321**

***Then*, for trip trade, use these entries:**

A Trades away sequence 123 to **B** **HTS/A/123/13SEP**

B Trades away sequence 456 to **A** **HTS/B/456/13SEP/CA**

Or for flight attendants,

B Trades away sequence 456 to **A** **HTS/B/456/13SEP**

***OR* to one-way drop** to another crewmember:

A Drops sequence 123 to **B** **HTO/A/123/13SEP/UNC**

Move DFPs as necessary (**HTMD**), exit trip trade mode **HZ**

With Open Time: Enter trip trade mode **HT**

***Then*, to drop to open time, use this entry:**

Drop sequence 123 to open time **HTO/A/123/13SEP/PVD**

***OR* to pick up sequence from open time use this entry:**

Pick up sequence 124 from open time **HTO/B/124/14SEP**

***OR* to trade with open time, use both entries above.**

Move DFPs (**HTMD**) and exit, as above **HZ**

Moving Duty-Free Periods

Duty-Free Periods (DFPs) may be manually moved by dropping and adding them using separate entries. Each DFP must be dropped, then added on another date. Manual DFP movement takes the place of the **HTMD** entry in the sequence of the actual trip trade mode commands above. These entries manually change duty-free periods.

NOTE: *Duty free periods can only be moved through these entries while entering a trip trade. At other times, you must contact Crew Schedule to move duty-free periods, or use* **HIDFP** *entries (see below).*

HTD/<A or B>/<DFP>/<Date> Delete DFP **HTD/A/24/20MAY**

HTA/<A or B>/<Date> Add DFP **HTA/A/48/15JUN**

Use either **A** or **B** in each entry, depending on which crewmember's record is affected. Deleted and added DFPs must be of the same value, i. e. a 24 must be substitute for a 24. To combine a 24 and a 48 into a 72, you can remove the 24 and 48, then add the 72.

Duty-free periods may be moved without being in trip trade mode with the following entries:

HIDFP/<Month MMM>/R Remove all DFPs for remainder of current month. **HIDFP/JUL/R**

HIDFP*/<Month MMM> Display DFPs as currently scheduled for the specified month. **HIDFP*/JUL**

NHR/<DFP>/<Date DDMMM> Remove current DFP. Allowable DFPs are **24**, **48**, **72**, or **96**. **NHR/96/13JUL**

NHA/<DFP>/<Date DDMMM> Add DFP (**24**, **48**, **72**, or **96**). A DFP may start immediately following trip debrief, or at midnight of the date specified. **NHR/96/13JUL**

HZ Close DFP adjustment session. No changes will be retained without the **HZ** entry. To exit without saving, enter **IG**.

HIDIR/HELP/CP/TT/LDFP Legal Duty Free Period tables displayed for domestic flying.

HIDIR/HELP/CP/TT/IRSV Legal Duty Free Period tables displayed for international reserve.

RF3200ATTOT Summary of how many crewmembers are using trip trades successfully.

Personal Mode General Information

HI1 Current Month Activity Record

HI2 Previous or next month's activity record

HI3 Current Trip Sequence

HI4 Sequence Display of last sequence

HI5 Sequence Display, next sequence

HI6 & **HI6A** Electronic Mail and print functions—no longer available outside Crew CheckIn Application or web page.

HI7 Address & phone numbers currently in Sabre system

HI8 Crew base & seniority data

HI9 License data CP

HI*9 Display Equipment Qualifications FA

HI*9/<C or **M>** Summary Of Equipment Qualifications; **C**– Current qualifications; **M** – Medical Data Only CP **HI*9/M**

HI*9/<Equipment>/<Seat> Equipment qualifications, detailed and expanded for specific equipment CP **HI*9/737/CA**

HI10 Vacation and planned absences

HI11/<Month> Miscellaneous Expenses **HI11/JUN**

HI12/<Month> Sequence Expenses **HI12/SEP**

HI13 View Sequence Duty Period messages FA

HI14/<Station>-<DDMMMYY> Record airport special qualification currency date . CP **HI14/EGE-13SEP18**

HI15/<Flight#>/<Date>/<Station> Nicknames of flight crew; Same display as NST, but you must be signed in to your personal mode to use this version. **HI15/333/13SEP/ORD**

HI16 Re-display Today's e-mail messages (CCI only)

HI17/<Station>/<#Minutes> Enter driving time in minutes to airport **HI17/DFW/25**

HI17/<Station> Delete stored airport driving time **HI17/DFW**

HI18/<Type Travel Doc>* Enter US or foreign passport or visa. Travel Doc types include **US** (US Passport), **VI** (foreign visa), and **AR** (alien registration). This entry brings up a form into which document data may be entered. **HI18/US***

Online Note: *Using non-SABRE terminals through the Internet, a configuration change may be required. From the Sabre* **Configuration** *menu* ( ), *select* **"Show Host Carriage Returns."** *The online forms should then work properly*

Note: *End* **HI18** *transaction with* **ET** *entry to save data.*

HI18/VI*/<Country> Enter foreign visa, for country listed. France is used in the example **HI18/VI*/FR**

For a list of acceptable country codes, enter **COUNTRY**

Note: *End* **HI18** *transaction with* **ET** *entry to save data.*

HI19/<Month>/II Change Options II status FA **HI19/JUN/II**

HI22 Special Training Class Completion List

HI22/<2 Digit List Number> Special training class **HI22/27**

HI22/57 Phone Number Release Authorization

HI23/<License Type>/<Issue Date>/<License#>/ <Free Text> Update license data. Allowable license types:

FE—Flight Engineer **AP**—ATP rating
CP—Commercial Pilot **ME**—A & P mechanic rating

HI23/AP/13SEP94/12345678/FAA^INSP^SMITH

HI23/<License Type > Delete license data **HI23/ME**

HI24A/<Month>/<Date DDMMM>/<Date DDMMM> Sequence activity–all flights in sequence; (dates optional) **HI24A/MAY/01MAY/15MAY**

HI24E/<Month>/<Date DDMMM>/<Date DDMMM> Sequence Activity–last flight of sequence; (dates optional) **HI24E/MAY/01NOV/15NOV**

HI25/<Date> Available reserve count junior and senior to in your category, on reserve on the day specified. CP **HI25/13SEP**

HI30/<Month>/S Set Monthly 30 Hour Waiver FA **HI30/SEP/S**

HI33/<Division D or I>/<Date DDMMM>/<Short or Long> Reserve list—see page 31. **HI33/D/9/S**

HI*E/<Equipment>/<Seat>/<VAR> Detailed equipment qualifications; **<VAR>** is **O**-Original; **R**-Recurrent; **E**-Experience; **N**-International Navigation CP **HI*E/320/CA/E**

HI<Equipment>/<DDMMMYY> Record a landing on date specified. CP **HI787/13SEP18**

HI<Equipment>H/<DDMMMYY>> Record a landing on date specified. CP **HI737H/13SEP18**

HIB/*/S Display Secondary Bid Ballot FA

HIB/S Secondary Bid Ballot Mode FA

HICAT3<Equipment>/<DDMMMYY> Record autoland on date specified. CP **HI777/13SEP18**

HICLAIM Pay Claim System FA

HICTL/<Set or Unset> Set or unset centerline thrust restriction designation for FAA multi-engine rating FA **HICTL/U**

HIDEP Revenue Deposit System FA

HID View division qualifications CP

HIDIR Personal Mode Master Directory

HIDIR/HELP/CP/HELP Hot Path Help Information CP

HIDIR/HTL/<City 1st Letter>/<Station> Hotel pickup, station code and phone information **HIDIR/HTL/K/MCI**

HIE* Display recurrent training requested-avoidance dates

HIEA/<Date–DDMMM>–<Date>/<Date>/<Date> Recurrent training requested-avoidance. Up to 4 dates; range is specified with the – key. **HIEA/13SEP–15SEP/19SEP/27SEP**

HIED/<DDMMM>–<DDMMM>/<DDMMM>/<DDMMM> Delete training avoidance request **HIED/13SEP–15SEP**

HIER Acknowledge Recurrent Training

HIFIT/123456/<Flight#>/<Date>/<Station>/<Dep Time *Optional*> CP Certify Fit for Duty for next leg of sequence. Use departure time for duplicate flight number if needed. **HIFIT/123456/64/DFW** or **HIFIT/123456/64/DFW/1055**

HIH/<DDMMM> Cancel Layover Hotel room **HIH/13SEP**

HIHTL/<Flight #>/<Date DD>/<Origination Station>/ Hotel information & voucher printout. See page 20 for description. **HIHTL/333/13/DFW** or **HIHTL/333/13/DFW**

HIM/<DDMMMYY>/<Class>/<Doctor's Name> Enter Medical; Class = 1 Or 2. **HIM/11JUL94/2/SMITH**

HIMAX Individual monthly maximum legal time

HIPH/<H, T or B>/<Phone #> Change phone numbers, home (**H**), travel (**T**) or business (**B**) **HIPH/B/8172831234**

HIPVD PVD Help information and instructions

HISEND Message Sending Capability

HISS/<Employee#>/<Passcode> Sign in for standby FA **HISS/123456/MYCODE01**

HITG/<Date>/<Date>/<Station> List available and closed classes FA **HITG/01SEP/30SEP/ORD**

HITH/<Date>/<Date>/<Station> List closed training classes FA **HITH/01SEP/30SEP/ORD**

PER

3 Personal Mode

HITJ/<Date>/<Date>/<Station> List available classes FA
HITJ/01SEP/30SEP/ORD

HIU/<Class Number> Add your name to a class FA **HIU/94D**

HIU/<Class Number>/S Add your name to the Standby List for a class FA **HIU/94D/S**

HIV/<Class Number> View Class Roster FA **HIV/94D**

HIX Sign Out of Personal Mode

3A. Personal Mode—Pilots

This section contains pilots-only personal mode entries.

Schedule Enhancement Period (SEP) Bidding

Functions formerly accomplished using this method are now done through the Trip Trade System (TTS). See detailed instructions on AA Pilots web site, Scheduling tab.

Standing Bid-Preferences & Displacements

Bid Status And Relative Bid Result Entries

3* Standing bid currently in system

3BR Display monthly bid results 50 senior & junior to you at your crew base

3XP Bid results with same bid status. (*Enhanced display available at APA internet web site is more detailed. See page 57.*)

3I/Y Set agreement to exceed max.

3I Unset agreement to exceed max.

3K/<Base>/<Seat>/<Equipment>/<Division>/R Reinstatement/entitlement count (*only*) **3K/DFW/CA/767/I/R**

3U/<Base>/<Seat>/<Equipment>/<Division> Relative status, same category & base (*only*) **3U/ORD/CA/777/D**

3NPP/ Display potential bid preferences

Standing Bid Preference Entries

3P/<Base>/<Seat>/<Equipment>/<Division> Add Standing Bid preference **3P/DFW/FO/320/D**

3P/CANCEL^<Number> Delete standing bid **3P/CANCEL^5**

3P/CANCEL^<Number>^TO^<Number> Delete a range of standing bid preferences **3P/CANCEL^5^TO^8**

3P/MOVE^<Number>^TO^<Number> Reorder standing bid preference **3P/MOVE^4^TO^2**

Standing Bid Displacement Preference Entries

3D/<Base>/<Seat>/<Equipment>/<Division>/P Add bid for Standing displacement; **<Division>** is domestic (**D**) or international (**I**). **/P** suffix indicates "paid move only," and may be left off if desired. **3D/ORD/FO/767/I/P**

3D/CANCEL^<Number> Delete standing displacement preference, Use **<Number>^TO^<Number>** a to delete a range of preferences. **3D/CANCEL^3** or **3D/CANCEL^2^to^4**

3D/MOVE^<Number>^TO^<Number> Reorder Standing Displacement **3D/MOVE^3^TO^1**

Reserve Flying Entries

This section contains entries especially helpful to pilots who are on reserve. Makeup entries are included below as well.

HI25/<Date> Display available reserve count. Shows number senior and junior to you on specified date. **HI25/13SEP**

HI33/<Division>/<Date DDMMM>/<Variance Group>/ <Starting Seniority *Optional***>/ <Ending Seniority** *Optional* **>/<Time Group** *Optional***>** Display 7-day reserve list, including current projections and availability. Divisions are **D**omestic or **I**nternational; Variance group is **L**ong (10-hour grouping) or **S**hort (3-hour grouping.) Variance group or number of days can be specified. **HI33/D/08NOV/L///2**

To specify seniority or range, enter in appropriate block.

Display reserves **beginning** with specified seniority number who are in 10-hour time group 1 **HI33/I/8NOV/L/5000//1**

Display reserves **ending** with specified seniority number in all time groups **HI33/I/8NOV/L//5400**

Display reserves **ending** at specified seniority number who are also in time group 1 **HI33/I/8NOV/L//5550/1**

Display reserves **within the specified seniority range** in all time groups **HI33/I/8NOV/L/5200/5400**

To see open trips, including which ones you are currently legal to fly, see **HIFIND**, **N3** and **N4** coes in the following sections.

Reserve Preference Ballot

The reserve preference ballot is a DECS personal mode subset which is entered by the command **HIRPB**

The following menu comes up as a result of this command:

```
MAIN MENU     -RSV PREFERENCES FOR 123456 SMITH JP

  1. OBTAIN YOUR ASSIGNMENT
  2. DISPLAY YOUR RSV STATUS, SEQUENCE AND RAP PREFERENCES
  3. SEQUENCE BALLOT OPTIONS
  4. RAP BALLOT OPTIONS
  5. RESERVE STATUS OPTIONS
  Q. QUIT WORKING WITH RESERVE PREFERENCES
*** TO CONFIRM A SEQUENCE ENTER LINE NUMBER ***
-----------------------------------------------
**** ENTER YOUR DESIRED TRANSACTION OR Q TO QUIT ****
```

From this point, menu commands **1** through **5** are used to select and **Q** to quit.

Finding Sequences for Trip Trades or Pickup

Trip trades, pickups, drops, and postings can be done with the codes in this section. It is is divided into the activities needed to 1) find a trip and 2) pick up or trade for that trip. A help screen displays formats for most common codes, and is fairly easy to remember when you do not have this book with you. It is:

HITRIP Display trip trade help screen. Shows entry formats. Other codes (some displayed in **HITRIP**) are as follows:

HIFIND/<Day> Show legal open trips for user. Displays only the sequence number, unlike the N4 entry which shows much more (*see below.*) Displays sequences in or out of your division for which you are legal—will show domestic sequences even if you are currently in international division. **HIFIND/13**

Adding **DFP** to the end includes sequences that will require changing of duty free periods. Sequences which ***require*** DFP adjustment each have an asterisk (*) **HIFIND/13/DFP**

N3<Division>/<Station>/<Equipment>/<Position>/<Date>/<End Date *Optional***>** Display trips, including those already assigned out of open time, for specified division (**D** or **I**) and dates. **N3D/JFK/737/CA/13SEP/15SEP**

Leaving out **<Equipment>** code displays all trips for the base. **N3DO/DFW//CA/13SEP**

Adding a letter **O** after the **<Division>** (**D** or **I**) shows only open sequences. **N3DO/DFW/320/CA/13SEP**

N4<Division>/<Base>/<Equipment>/<Position>/<Date>/<Date *Optional***>** Display open and posted sequence lists. Shows hours legal for pickup, number of legs per day, layover cities, and navigation qualification needed to fly the trip. Asterisk (*) indicates not all information is shown due to space limitations. Second date, if shown, defines end of date range.

N4I/DFW/767/CA/13SEP or **N4I/DFW/767/CA/13/16**

Adding **L** after **<Division>** shows only trips for which you are legal. Only one day may be specified, like the **HIFIND** entry, but showing all the detail of the **N4** entry. **N4** Cannot find sequences which would be legal with a duty-free period shuffle. (See **HIFIND**, above.) **N4IL/DFW/767/FO/13SEP**

If no trip is found which solves your needs, the next best option is to find someone who holds a trip you would like, and ask that pilot to trade with you. To do this, you can look for a sequence in the bid sheet and use an HSS entry to find out who holds the trip.

N4T/<Sequence>/<Date> Display possible trips for trade with "red" status trip in your current schedule **N4T/3033/26JUL**

N4TL/<Sequence>/<Date> Display legal trips for trade with trip specified which is in your schedule. **N4TL/3033/26JUL**

HIQUAL/<Seat>/<Sequence>/<Date> Display qualifications required for specified sequence **HIQUAL/FO/123/13SEP**

HSS/<Seat>/<Sequence>/<Date> Sequence times and specifics **HSS/CA/3101/13**

Another option is HIBOARD, a listing board of trips pilots are trying to trade. You may be able to find a mutually agreeable trade through this method. It is fairly user-friendly. Simply type **HIBOARD** ENTER, and follow the instructions.

Note: *You need not be in personal mode to access open time entries, but pilot entries are grouped here, and F/A open time codes are on page 38.*

Makeup Flying List

HIHP/<Start Date>/<End Date> Add to makeup list **HIHP/13SEP/19SEP**

HIHP/<Start Date>/<End Date>/D Delete from makeup List **HIHP/13SEP/19SEP/D**

HIJV/<Start Date>/<End Date> Add to voluntary junior available list **HIJV/13SEP/19SEP**

HIJV/<Start Date>/<End Date>/D Delete from makeup voluntary junior list **HIJV/13SEP/19SEP/D**

NNV/<Date>/<Base>/<Seat>Display Voluntary Junior Availale list **NNV/25/LAX/CA**

Assessing Your Sequences

Not all of your sequence will be eligible for dropping. To determine which ones are, use the following code:

HISEQ Display status of all sequences currently held, either current or next month after bids close. Possible status indicators:

GREEN-Trip can be dropped or traded with any open sequence for which the crewmember is open and legal.

RED-Coverage is too low currently to allow drops. ***Trades are*** allowed under RED rules. Can trade for a trip which:

♦ Contains at least the same number of calendar days.

♦ Contains the same or more navigation qualifications as the trip dropped. **Note**: *Crew schedule can override the nav qual requirement depending on reserve coverage for that period.*

HOLD-System temporarily on hold for update of TTOT lights.

OFF-System is turned off for this.

CPA Management

CPA bank time payout is directed with the payout code, which specifies any legal amount in accordance with contract provisions.

HIPAYOUT/<Month>/<Time H.MM> Pay specified CPA time from 1 minute to 5 hours maximum **HIPAYOUT/FEB/2.30**

To cancel, re-enter with zero time. **HIPAYOUT/FEB/0.00**

HIDIR/CTRC/CPA Help file information regarding payout.

Self-Listing for Travel To & From Training

Travel to and from training may be scheduled or changed by individuals using personal mode. Travel to training is scheduled automatically, but pilots may cancel the listing and reschedule themselves using the entries below. Travel to training is A1, using code **A1D**. Travel on 48s during training and travel home at the end of training is A3, code **A3D**.

HIGOA/<Flight>/<Date>/<Seat>/<From>/<To>/<Travel Classification> List self for travel
HIGOA/333/15JUN/CA/ORD/DFW/A1D

HIGOR/<Flight>/<Date>/<Seat>/<From>/<To>/<Travel Classification> Cancel/Remove a listing for a flight
HIGOR/333/15JUN/CA/ORD/DFW/A3D

Limitations:

- ♦Ticketless deadhead listings can only be made on American Airlines flights–not American Eagle or other carriers.
- ♦Valid only for travel in the 48 contiguous states, not international.

3B. Personal Mode—Flight Attendants

This section contains personal mode entries which are available only to flight attendants. In addition, Personal Mode basic chapter 3 entries can also be used by flight attendants.

Speed Bid Option

The Speed Bid Option allows moving through the panels of the bidding menu quickly. It lets you move from one screen to the next without going to the main menu to choose the next transaction. To move directly to the next panel, type X followed by the number desired. For example, **X3** ENTER or **X8** ENTER. If you were in the **ADD/START PANEL** and wanted to go directly to the **BUDDY BID PANEL** number **10**, you would type **X10** ENTER. The Speed Bid Option only works from within a transaction.

If you are at the **MAIN MENU**, type only the transaction number to continue to the instruction panel. Then you may use the speed bid option again. This should save time when bidding.

Finding Sequences for Trip Trades or Pickup

The Trip-Trading Bulletin Board is one way to find trips. It is fairly user-friendly and may be used to find trips for drop or pick up To access,simply type **HIBOARD** ENTER, and follow the instructions. For open trips, you may also use the N3 entry.

N3<Division>/<Station>//<Start Date>/<End Date *Optional*>

Results in open trips on the date or range specified. **<Division>** is either **D** for Domestic or **I** for International

N3D/DFW//5JUL

Adding **O** after the **N3D** or **N3I** portion returns only open trips.

N3DO/DFW//5JUL or **N3IO/DFW//5JUL/7JUL**

If no trip is found, you can to find someone who holds a trip you would like, and ask them to trade with you. Use an HSS entry to find out who holds the trip for which you want to try to trade.

HSS/<Position>/<Sequence>/<Date> Sequence times and specifics **HSS/02/3101/13**

Trip Trades & Optional Exchange

If Flight Attendant **A** is trading the sequence, then Flight Attendant **B** will automatically be assigned to the sequence as optional exchange, and vice versa. If incorrect information is entered, three chances are allowed to correct the error. The following are used:

HIHP/<Start Date>/<End Date>/<MU or **II>** Add to Makeup or Option 2 List **HIHP/13SEP/19SEP/MU/D**

HIHP/<Start Date>/<End Date>/<MU or **II>/D** Delete from Makeup or Option 2 List **HIHP/13SEP/19SEP/MU**

Position Swaps

To change positions on the same sequence with another member of your crew, use the exact same entries as you use for trip trades. Those entries are listed in **HIDIR/HELP/FA/TT**

Note: *If you picked up the trip on Makeup, Optional Exchange or Reserve, you* ***will not*** *be able to swap positions unless Flight Service determines you are needed to work a Premium or Galley Position. In this case, Flight Service MOD must send a message to Crew Schedule for you.*

Triggering For Service Or Equipment Training

To trigger (request being scheduled) for training for equipment qualifications, such as 737 or 777, or for service qualifications, such as International Flagship Service (IFS) or 3-Class TransCon, or for Premium or Galley Training:

1. First, choose Option 11 on the HIB Main Menu.
2. Then, type in the code of the training for which you would like to "trigger." The codes you need to use are listed below:

   3.......... 3-Class TransCon **11**.......... IFS
   24......... Tokyo IFS **PPY**......... Premium
3. For equipment qualification training, use the equipment code.

Type **H** for Help while in the Trigger Menu.

Note: *ALL entries in chapter 3,* ***Personal Mode Entries****, are available to Flight Attendants. This chapter contains specific entries available* ***only*** *to flight attendants.*

FLT ATT PER

4. RES Codes

This chapter documents the Reservation mode (RES). But it is mostly geared to non-revenue travel. So, following an introduction to the ACS entries (Automated Check-in System), the layout of the chapter follows a logical progression of

- Finding the flight you want .... ***Schedule***
- Checking the availability of seats .... ***Availability***
- "Flight-Listing" yourself .... ***Listing***
- Verifying the listing......... ***Did you you list yourself correctly?***
- Checking the Airport Standby List to check your likelihood of getting on the desired flight .... ***Day of travel information***
- Other nice-to know information about your destination
- Other miscellaneous helpful information in RES.

In the process of exploring these areas, you will find yourself getting much more familiar with the RES Mode in general.

Signing In to RES

A detailed description of signing in is found in Chapter 1, General Sabre Information. See page 9 for information on signing in to RES.

Related DECS Codes

Where appropriate, a few DECS codes are thrown in where they provide especially helpful information for the non-revenue traveler exploring the world of Sabre information. They are found at the end of their respective sections under the heading above.

Note: *For all entries in this section, substitute* [*for* ⊠ *when* Online.

Automated Check-in System (ACS) Entries

The ACS entries encompass most RES codes which begin with the letter **G**. These codes make a wealth of information available through the use of only a few entries. That is the good news. The bad news is that decoding the entries is not easy in many cases. This section will offer decoding examples for a few of the key entries. Others generally follow the layouts found in these examples. Additional entries and codes can be found using the **FOCUS** system entry **F*ACS**. The ACS system brings more information to the screen with fewer keystrokes. Again, all entries in this section which begin with the letter **G** are considered ACS entries.For additional information on the **FOCUS** system, see page 53.

All entries used in this book have been checked and will work either from a dedicated Sabre terminal or from a home computer via modem using PCFOS.

Availability Entries

This section contains codes to help you find what flights are *actually listed on a given day between two stations.*

1<Date><Dep Station><Arr Station> Next scheduled AA flights, including connections **113SEPRSWORD**

This is a basic informational entry. A typical entry might result in:

```
198 F7 Y7 B5 M3 Q3 RSWRDU 8 N 622P 811P 738 D 0 XJ
382 F1 Y0 Q0 M0 Q0 ORD    6 N 856P 959P 320 D 0
```

Decoded, the information is as follows:

Flight **198** has at least **7** seats left in **F**irst class from its authorized overbooking level. It has at least **7** seats left in full fare coach (**Y**), **5** seats left on coach fare **B**, and **3** seats each for fares **M** and **Q**. The **RSW** to **RDU** on-time performance level is **8** (9 is perfect). *This* is a non-smoking flight (**N**), departing at **622P**M, and arriving **811P**M. The aircraft scheduled is a Boeing **738** (737-800 series), is a dinner flight (**D**), has zero stops (**0**) and does not operate on Saturday (**XJ**). It connects with AA **382**, which is very full. Availability never shows more than 7 seats, regardless of number actually available. A number less than 7 represents the number of seats ***actually left*** from authorized overbooking level. Flight 382 has only **1** seat left in **F**irst class. It leaves **RDU** at **856P**M and arrives **ORD** at **959P**M. The scheduled aircraft is a **320**.

The following codes provide information in a similar format, with various options for included flights:

1<Date DDMMM><Dep Station><Arr Station><TIME> Same as above, but departing after specified **<Time>** (12-hour format—**A** for AM, **P** for PM; so 7:00PM=**7P**). Shows available flights, either AA or Eagle. **113SEPSTLORD7A**

1* More scheduled flights after above entry

1*OA Flight availability–other than AA & American Eagle.

1*<Time> Change specified time, or specify time if none was specified previously. For flights leaving close to 2PM: **1*2P**

1<Station> Flights through the specified station which connect the initially specified departure and arrival stations. **1BNA**

1R<Date><Time *Optional*> Show return flights on specified date. **1R13JAN** or **1R13JAN7A**

1‡<# Days> Availability as currently requested, on specified number of days *after* the date of the by previous entry **1‡3**

1–<# Days> Availability as currently requested, on specified number of days *before* the date in previous entry. **1–3**

S<Dep Station><Arr Station> American Airlines schedules between two stations **SDFWORD**

2<Flight#> Flight status information–similar to DECS FIL entries, showing scheduled vs. actual flight progress. **2333**

1*ORIG Return to first **1*** screen, i.e., before **1R** entries, etc.

Related DECS Codes

26A/<Dep Station>/<Arr Station>/<Date> Flights scheduled non-stop between stations **26A/BNA/ORD/13**

26K/<Dep Station>/<Arr Station>/<Date> Connecting flights scheduled between stations. (Includes some connection possibilities RES will not list.) **26K/BNA/SEA/13**

26B/<Dep Station>/<Arr Station>/<Date> Both direct *and* connecting flights between stations **26B/BNA/ORD/13**

Non-Revenue Travel

Seat Availability

VIL<Flight#>/<Date><Station> Display seat availability for a flight. Compare the left hand **AC** column (aircraft capacity) to the **SS** column (actual seats sold). **VIL54/15SEPORD**

```
54 ORD
F  AC 14    AU 14  SA 12  SS  2
C  AC 36    AU 42  SA  0  SS 42
Y  AC 164    AU 175  SA 17  SS 158
B          AU 165  SA  7
M          AU 160  SA  2
V          AU 155  SA -3
Z          AU 154  SA -4
Q          AU 153  SA -5    SP CL
```

AC–Aircraft Capacity, **F**=first class, **C**=business, **Y**=coach. Letters **B**, **M**, **V**, **Z** & **Q** are discounted-fare coach seats, and are included in the coach total.

AU–Total Seats **AU**thorized for sale, including overbooking. Compare this to **AC** (aircraft capacity) to approximate the historic percentage of no-show passengers. **AU** numbers much higher than capacity (**AC**) indicate a high level of no shows. Numbers close to capacity indicate the flight normally has few no shows. Overbooking in First Class is not authorized.

SA–Seats **A**vailable. Overbooking level minus seats sold. This is ***not*** a good indicator of seat availability.

SS–Seats **S**old (actual) Compare this number to **AC** to see how many seats are really left. Above, coach is 164-158=6 seats

AS–Actual Seats **S**old on International flights (not shown in this example). Use this number <u>instead of SS</u>. **SS** on international flights does not include passengers from "funnel flights".

VNR<Flight#>/<Date><Station> Display non-revenue meal listings on a specific flight. **VNR295/15SEPDFW**

The resulting display for this entry would look as follows:

```
295 DFW
AVAIL   F 12   C  0   Y 17
NONREVS     5      1      3
```

From the **VIL** example, note the airplane holds 14 in first class, 36 in business and 164 in coach. Seats sold are 2F, 42C and 158Y. Therefore, first is open, business is oversold, and coach has 6 seats left. Discount fares B, M, V, Z and Q mean nothing, since they are part of coach. Since **AU** numbers are close to **AC** (capacity), most booked passengers historically show up for this flight. Using the **VNR** entry, the response shows 5 Non-Revs are flight listed for first class, 1 for business class and 3 for coach. Therefore, all 5 Non-Revs will get on in first class since a few Advantage passengers will upgrade (but it will be close) and the other 4 should get on in coach.

G*<Flight#>/<Date DDMMM *Optional***><City** *Optional***>** Display flight status record; shows the number of authorized passenger seats, jumpseats, booking levels, and number of passengers checked in and ON'd. Also shows meal or beverage counts and if applicable, passenger limit restrictions and unaccommodated passenger notice. **G*333**

Add departure date or city **G*123/21JUN** or **G*123ORD**

Add date ***and*** city **G*123/21JUNORD**

For a sample listing of the **G*** information format and what it means, see the chart on the next page.

```
                                (1)                  (2)                     (3)        (4)
    G*86/5OCTORD«
    AA        86   5OCT    ORD L8       505P  777 16/37/194   OPENCI      BDG
                 F     C    Y     TO LHR                   (5) SEE US LIST -03
 (6)AUTH        15    37  194                             (18) JUMPSEATS
(7)->BOOKED     14    36  172                                ACTUAL W-2 X-12
 (8)AVAIL        1     1   22                                IN USE W-0 X-11
                             (15)
(9)->THRU RV     0     0    0 NR  0     0    0 ASSIGN     F      C      Y
(10)LCL   RV    15    37  166 NR  0     0    0 RESTRICT   DSR    A6P    A6P
                             (16)
(11)->LCL  ON*  14    32  118 TK  0     0    2 MEALS      15¥ 0  37¥ 0  189¥
(12)TTL  ON*    14    32  118 ET 14    32  116 SETUPS     15     37     194
(13)->TLOB      15    37  166 (17)
(14)PLAN        15    37  168                  SEE PULL-  18
```

1 Planned departure gate
2 @—Indicates a change of equipment.
3 **OPENCI**—Flight status. For status change explanation, see FOCUS record **F*ACS/FLIGHT/STATUS/CHANGE**
4 **BDG**—Flight boarding indicator. Gate agent sets this when boarding begins. See **F*ACS/BOARDING/INDICATOR**
5 **LIST**—Indicates flight has unaccommodated passengers and/or passengers whose seats have been changed due to equipment change. The number is the number of passengers on the list.
6 **AUTH**—Maximum number of seats (by compartment) which may be occupied at departure time, not including crew rest or broken seats. Authorized count can be changed by gate agents. See **F*ACS/CHANGE/AUTH**
7 **BOOKED**—Total number of seats sold on this flight leg, including both local and through-booked passengers.
8 **AVAIL**—Seats available to sell; **AUTH** minus **BOOKED**
9 **THRU RV**—Count of revenue and positive space passengers traveling through on this flight.
10 **LCL RV**—Count of local boarding passengers who have been issued boarding passes, including positive space.
11 **LCL ON**—Local boarding passengers ON'd, incl. non-rev.
12 **TTL ON**—Count of all passengers ON'd, local and through
13 **TLOB**—Count of all issued local & through boarding passes
14 **PLAN**—Projected final passenger count as calculated (***projected***) by load planning agent.
15 **NR**—Line 1: Through non-rev count, excluding positive space
Line 2: Local non-rev count, excluding positive space
16 **TK**—Total ON count of ticketed passengers.
17 **TT**—Total ON count of ticketless passengers.
18 **JUMPSEATS**: **ACTUAL**—Number of jumpseats on this aircraft; **IN USE**—Number of working crew and passengers assigned to a jumpseat

Flight Listing

You must list yourself for the flight you intend to use at least 60 minutes before departure. Flight listing (formerly called a *meal* listing) may be accomplished through JetNet, Sabre AVRS, or reservation agents available at 1-800-433-7300. Most people prefer to make reservations through JetNet. Entries below allow you to do it directly from SABRE via an airport terminal or PC FOS access.

Note: *Authorized travelers **must** be pre-registered through JetNet before listing through any of these sources.*

There are two ways to list through the Sabre network.

◆ **Method 1:** Direct listing, using the codes below:

Ø<Flight><Class><Date DDMMM><Dep Station><Arr

Station>MM<Number Listing> Initiate listing steps. Next three must be done to complete the listing. Creates a Passenger Name Record (PNR). **02366Y13SEPDFWORDMM3**

E*‡<Employee Number> Specify employee's list of authorized travelers. **E*‡123456** or when Online **E*'123456**

The entry brings up a list of authorized travelers from which you can select the appropriate individuals. It will look something like this:

```
RES > E*$123456
AA00123456 SMITH,RICHARD TKTG-ELECTRONIC
AMR EMPLOYEE              DOM COACH FEE WAIVED /5YR/
BUS-A12  A9-Y             CO SEN DATE-04/26/1992
TVLR NAME                 PERS    AA20  OAL JUMPSEAT
---- -------------------------- ----  --- --------
   1 SMITH/RICHARD     D2,D1      Y       Y   FDJ AA
   2 SMITH/GAIL        D2,D1      Y       Y
   3 SMITH/ANDREW      D2,D1      Y       Y
   4 SMITH/MATTHEW     D2,D1      Y       Y
   5 SMITH/JONATHAN    D2,D1      Y       Y
   6 SMITH/ARTHUR      D2,D2P     Y       Y
   7 JONES/DANIEL      D3         Y       Y
   8 JONES/SUSIE       D3         Y       Y
```

E*‡–<1st Passenger>,<2ND Passenger> Identify line numbers of passengers traveling *in the same travel category.*

E*‡–1 or **E*‡–1,3,5** or from Online **E*'–1 or E*'–1,3,5**

7EM–<Travel Category> specify the category in which the party will travel (A11, D1, D2, D3,etc.) **7EM–D2**

Note: *If passengers are traveling in different priority categories, i.e. D1 & D2, or D2 & D3, You must create separate PNRs.*

9<Area Code & Phone Number or PWCT> Phone contact information. The optional entry **PWCT** means "passenger will contact" the company. Depending on workload, a non-rev traveller may not be called. **98172831234** or **9PWCT**

6P Identifies the listing agent (**6P** means you listed yourself)

ET End Transaction. Closes listing; saves the Passenger Name Record (PNR.) The response should be "`OK <PNR Number>`." The `<PNR Number>` will be a 6-letter code identifying the record. See "Working with the PNR Record," page 48.

To summarize these entries, a typical set of commands follows.

RES Entries	Entries (if Different) Online
E*‡123456 ENTER (*A list results*)	**E*'123456**
E*‡–1,3,5 ENTER (*Numbers from list*)	**E*'–1,3,5**
7EM–D2 ENTER	Same
Ø891F05JUNORDDFWMM3	Same
9PWCT ENTER	Same
6P ENTER	Same
ET ENTER	Same

◆ **Method 2:** Listing directly from an availability check is another method of listing. In this method, you check flight schedule and seat availability using one of the "**1...**" codes. An entry such as **12MARORDPB** might bring up the following display:

```
2MAR FRI   ORD/CST     PBI/ESTA1
1   744 F7 Y7 B7 H7 M7 Q7 ORDRDU 7 N   620A   914A D10
2   273 F1 Y7 B7 H7 M7 Q7 PBI      5 N 1000A 1150A 72S
3 1288 F5 Y0 H0 B0 M0 Q0 ORDPBI 7 N 1020A   350P 320
```

From this screen, you may list using the following codes:

Ø<Number Listing><1st Leg Class><Line#> <2nd Leg Class><Line#>MM List number of people specified on each leg in the previous display. Example lists two people on flight 744, connecting to RDU flight 273. **Ø2F1F2MM**

The codes needed to complete the listing process are the same as the ones above for names, (**E*‡** and **E*‡–)** phone number (**9+**), and travel category (**7EM–**) entries, then **6P** and **ET**.

◆ **JetNet Entries for Non-Rev Travel**

To use the JetNet web site for non-rev travel, use these steps:

- Go to **www.jetnet.aa.com** and log on
- From the JetNet home page, select the **TRAVEL** tab at the top
- From the JetNet Travel page, select the **Non-Rev Travel Planner** tab at the left side of the page
- Then select the appropriate link for availability, listing, etc.

Entering Round Trips in a Single PNR

To group connecting legs or a round trip in one PNR, list all legs before closing the PNR with the **ET** entry. This groups travel plans so agents can see that a passenger checking in has a connecting flight. This will also help to get bags transferred properly.

Non-Rev Status: Am I Getting on the Flight?

G*L<Flight#>/<Date><Station>/PALL Airport Standby List. **<Date>** optional for present date.

G*L123BNA/PALL or **G*L123/13SEPBNA/PALL**

To display only passengers who have not yet been given boarding passes, use only the suffix **P**.

G*L123BNA/P or **G*L123/13SEPBNA/P**

Adding ***H** will also show a passenger's check-in time for the priority list. **G*L123/13SEPBNA/PALL*H**

A sample listing follows with the decoding follows:

```
       1   2                     3    4
AA    436 05OCT    DFW C16      400P  737    PRIORITY LIST
        6 7 8                       9 10 11 12        13  14 15
5  1    *UPG2T RANKIN    CHARL       Y  X FLL       8A    1
T  2    -DRX   HICKEY    JAMES       F    FLL       5B    2
   3    -D1    PURYEAR   HERB   AJ2 F     FLL      13B    1
T  4     D2T   COFFMAN   MICHA       Y    FLL     1408    NB FDJ AA
T  5     D2PT  SMITH     CAROL       F    FLL             NB
```

1. Flight Number
2. Planned Departure Gate
3. Departure Time
4. Aircraft Type
5. Through Indicator
6. Priority List Line Number
7. Boarding Pass Issued (*) or Passenger ON (–)
8. Priority Code
9. Group Code
10. Booked Class of Service
11. Desired Class of Service
12. Flight Segment Destination Code
13. Seat Assignment *or* Transfer to Flight Number
14. Number of Bags Checked
15. Priority List Remarks

G*L<Flight#>/<Date><Station>/<Suffix> Information on a specific flight. Some of the allowable suffixes are below. For a complete list, see **F*ACS/EDIT**. Codes may be combined as in the following examples:

G*L123/13SEPDFW/UNMR or **G*L123/13SEPDFW/AC/BP**

*	Boarding pass but not ON
—	Passenger on board
AA	Passenger at the airport
AC	Add/collect information
ADM	Admirals club member
AD	Regular aadvantage
AF	Free ticket
AG	Aadvantage gold
AP	Aairpass
ARMD	Armed (SS)
AVIH	Animal in hold
BLND	Blind (SS)
BP	Boarding pass issued
BX	Passenger with pre-reserved seat or boarding pass
BT	Bag tag issues
CHD	Child, between 2 and 11 years
CLUB	Club access
CF	Change fee
CLE	Baggage cleared via CTX/EDS
CLT	Baggage cleared by trace detection
CLP	Baggage cleared by physical search
CLD	Baggage cleared by canine search
CL	Displays all cleared passengers, but not how they were cleared
CM	Passenger comments in PNR
CS	Codeshare passenger
DG	Downgrade
DEAF	Deaf (SS)
DEPA	Deportee, accompanied (SS)
DEPU	Deportee, unaccompanied (SS)
EP	Executive platinum
ET	Electronic ticket
EOB	Edifact outbound
EIB	Edifact inbound
ESCT	Officer escorting prisoner (SS)
FQTV	Other airline frequent traveler
FV	Full fare revenue passenger
HAND	Handcuffed prisoner (SS)
IB	Passenger has inbound connection
INF	Passenger traveling with infant
LF	Ticket lifted

LANG	Language assistance needed (SS)
MEDA	Medical clearance required (SS)
MAAS	Meet and assist (SS)
NS	No show
OB	Passenger has outbound connection
ON	Passenger onboard
OS	Oversale
OW	OneWorld top tier
OXYG	Oxygen (SS)
P	Priority list: unaccommodated passengers only
PALL	Priority list: all passengers
PETC	Pet in cabin
PL	AAdvantage platinum
PM	Premium passenger, includes aadvantage gold, platinum, aairpass or full fare revenue
PR	Prereserved seat
PRI	Passengers from priority list in order
PSPT	Passport information added
PCTC	Personal contact information
RV	Revenue
SC	Security checked
SM	Special meal
SP	Selectee passenger profile
SS	Support services list (SS)
TP	Tpi security tag
TWOV	Transit without visa (SS)
TX	Through list
UG	Upgrade
US	Unhonored seats list
USH	Unhonored seats history
UY	AAdvantage upgrade from coach
UC	AAdvantage upgrade from business
WX	Exempt from domestic PPBM

(SS) Special Service List

Working with the Passenger Name Record (PNR)

The PNR is created by making a flight listing (see **ET** entry description, page 45.) It identifies the itinerary of a traveler or group of travelers whose reservations were made at the same time. Viewing the PNR for is a good way to verify the listing has been made properly. You may use the following codes to view the PNR, and if appropriate, verify your special meal request.

***<Flight>/<Date>–<Last Name>** Display passenger record.
<Date> Optional for flight today. Today: ***333-JOHNSON**
or for other specified date: ***333/13SEP–JOHNSON**

***<Line Number>** If more than one "Johnson" is listed for the flight, a display of all listed "Johnson's" results. Select the proper one by specifying the line with this entry. ***2**

***<Passenger Name Record>** Open and display Passenger Name Record (PNR). ***SKCBGY**

ET End Transaction and close the PNR record

__Note__: *Additional possibilities for opening an existing PNR are contained in the discussion of cancellations below.*

Canceling the Flight Listing

You may also cancel the listing using the PNR. The company plans a meal for listed first class non-revenue travelers, so failure to cancel the listing could waste a meal and make the company assume the cost of providing it. You may cancel a listing with the following entries:

***<Passenger Name Record>** Open and display Passenger Name Reservation (PNR). If multiple travelers are in the record, each will be numbered ***SKCBGY**

X<Number of Passenger to be Canceled> The line number of the passenger to be canceled would be entered in the variable portion of the entry. **X2**

6P Identifies you as the agent making changes to the listing

IG Ignore any changes to the PNR.

ET End Transaction and close the PNR.

You may also use one of the following methods to open the PNR if you do not have the PNR transaction code.

<u>Alternate Method 1</u>. Make an availability listing "**1...**" Specify the line for the flight leg to be canceled using this with code:

****<Line #>–<Name>** Select a PNR by specifying the flight and passenger name ****2–SMITH**

Codes following are as above, from "**X...**" on.

<u>Alternate Method 2.</u> Use this if you know the flight number:

***<Flight>/<Date>–<Name>** Opens PNR ***1744/13JAN–DOE**

XI Cancel all itinerary segments (or **X<Line#>** to cancel individual segments) then **4EMPL**, **6P** & **ET** entries. **XI** or **X2**

‡FINISH OR IGNORE‡ For any of the above methods, if you open the PNR you must use the **ET** entry to <u>E</u>nd the <u>T</u>ransaction, or <u>I</u> to <u>I</u>gnore it. Entering other non-PNR entries without the ET entry results in the error message ‡FINISH OR IGNORE‡. Type **I** ENTER to ignore the changes or **ET** ENTER to process the changes, sign out of RES or perform other entries.

Fare Information

RES

The following codes are an introduction to finding fares on AA and other airlines.

FQ<Dep Station><Arr Station><Date> Fares on AA between city pair, both available and filled. **FQDFWLIT13OCT**

Adding **<Date><Year>** before and after the stations and **EX** to the end displays past fares (up to 60 days in the past.) **FQ15OCT16DFWORD15NOV16EX**

Adding suffix **–*J‡<Airline Code>** shows joint fare for AA & specified airline. Some fares use **<City>** instead of **<Station>**, i.e. **NYC** for **LGA**. **FQDFWNYC13JAN–*J‡DL**

Add **NLX–<Airline Code>** to display fares for carrier specified (example is Delta–**DL**) **FQORDDFW13OCTNLX–DL**

RD<Dep Station><Arr Station><Date><Fare Basis #> Display fare basis restrictions **RDORDDFW11MAYVE21N**

RD<Line #> Display travel and/or ticketing restrictions for any line number in the above display. **RD5**

Non-Revenue Service Charges

WR List of affiliate suffix codes allowable for next entry

WR<Station><Station><Station *Optional***>–<Affiliate Code>** Non-revenue service charges. Adding additional **<Station>** entries will include connecting flights in the charges. **WRDFWBDL–AA** or **WRORDRDUPBI–AA**

```
RES > WRDFWBOS-AA

D1/D2 EMP/RETIREE/SPOUSES/DOMESTIC PARTNER/DEP CHILD/PARENT/
REGISTERED COMPANION
AIRPORT        MILES       F-COST       J-COST       Y-COST    TRIP VALUE
DFW BOS        1,564        20.75                     7.67        66.86
                   DOM TAX   1.55                      .57
                   SEG TAX   2.50                     2.50
CHARGES  AND FEES           20.75                     7.67
  TAXES                      4.05                     3.07
  TOTAL        1,564        24.80    <-- D2 -->      10.74        66.86
AACHIEVERS POINTS           4,150                    1,534$

D3-OTHER PASS TRAVELERS
DFW BOS        1,564        66.86                    66.86
                   DOM TAX   5.01                     5.01
                   SEG TAX   2.50                     2.50
CHARGES  AND FEES           66.86                    66.86
  TAXES                      7.51                     7.51
  TOTAL        1,564        74.37    <-- D3 -->      74.37
AACHIEVERS POINTS          14,874                    14,874
```

Charges to be deducted from the following month's pay are found on the **TOTAL** line for the appropriate category of travel, i.e., first class, business or coach, and D2 or D3. Taxes do not need to be calculated separately. The full text resulting also breaks out costs for 5- and 25-year employees.

RES

Passenger-Related RES Code Information

Seating Information

G*N<Flight #>/<Date><Station>/<Last Name> Boarded passenger's assigned seat **G*N123/13SEPDFW/SMITH**

G*M<Flight#><Class><Dep Station><Arr Station>/S Cabin seat map; scheduled A/C, specified classes allowable are <u>F</u>irst Class, <u>B</u>usiness and <u>Y</u> (Coach). **G*M123BDFWORD/S**

G*S<Flight #>/<Date><Station>/<Last Name> Display passenger assigned to specific seat **G*S123/13SEPDFW/27A**

N*JETSA Aircraft fleet and seat configuration information

Meal Information

G*L<Flight#>/<Date><Station>/SM Special meals list; **<Date>** and **<Station>** are optional for current station and today's date **G*P333/SM**

PMM<Date>/<Flight>∧<Dep Station> Meal count (revenue and Non-Rev) **PMM13JAN/333∧ORD**

AAdvantage Reward Miles

V*<Flight> Mileage awarded on flight specified. **V*333**

Hub & Connection Information

G*<Flight>/<Date><City>/<Suffix> Display flight data in various categories. Suffix codes include the following:

/CPI List connecting passengers; includes AA and Eagle connections, departure time, gate and baggage zone. **G*453/21JUNDFW/CPI**

/FD Names and phone contact for local agent and management personnel assigned to the flight; smoking, meal, video, crew rest seat data, special service counts and passenger limit restrictions. **G*123/21JUNORD/FD**

/PLM Passenger Load Manifest Information for flight . **G*453/21JUNDFW/PLM**

/R R-Text, passengers on flight **G*453/21JUNDFW/R**

PBI<Flight>/<Date><Dep Station> Displays inbound passengers' connecting flights **PBI333/13JANORD**

Helpful RES Information

Coding and Decoding Information

W/*<CODE> Display airline name for specified code **W/*BA**

W/–AL<Airline> Airline code, given name **W/–ALDELTA**

W/*<Station> Display airport for coded station **W/*RNO**

W/EQ*<CODE> Display airplane type information **W/EQ*777**

W/EQ–<COMPANY> List airplane types in code w/equipment-manufacturer **W/EQ–BOEING**

W/–AP<Airport Name> Find city for airport named; Code returns: "OMA EPPLEY FIELD OMAHA NE" **W/–APEPPLEY**

W/–CC<City Name> Station abbreviation for state in which <**City Name**> is found **W/–CCRENO**

W/–CY<City Name> Distance to nearest airports with air service from <**City Name**>. If several possible matches, brings up a list of possible cities, which require the entry **W/–SL<Line #>** as in **W/–CYOMAHA** then **W/–SL1**

WM<Station><Station> Air miles between cities **WMDFWORD**

Time Entries

T*<Station> Local time at station specified **T*MIA**

T*<Station>/<S or **D>/<Zulu Time><L** or **Z>** Convert time between local and Greenwich Mean Time (GMT or **Z**ulu.) Input time either **S**tandard or **D**aylight savings time. Specifying **L** at end indicates the time you are entering is **L**ocal and you want **Z**ulu. Entering **Z** at the end returns local time. **T*LHR/S/1715Z**

†T Display time and date at HDQ (DFW) including Julian date

T⊠<Month>/<Year> Monthly calendar **T⊠OCT/16**

T⊠<Day> Display next four dates for the specified day of the week, i.e., for the next four Tuesdays, **T⊠TUE**

RES

T⊠<Day>/<Month> Display all calendar dates on which a specified day occurs in a specified month **T⊠TUE/OCT**

T⊠<Date 1>–<Date 2> Display the number of days between two dates **T⊠21SEP–25DEC** or **T⊠11SEP16–18JUN17**

T⊠<Date>‡<# of Days> Display date a specific number of days after entered date. For 30 days after 13 June, **T⊠13JUN‡30**

T⊠ET<Time 1><A or **P><Station 1>/<Date>–<Time 2><A** or **P><Station 2>/<Date>** Elapsed time between two times at any two stations. Time in **HHMM** format, where **HH**=hour and **MM**=minute. **A** or **P** Specifies AM or PM. Example is for time between 5:30AM at ORD and 1:30PM at LAX on March 1st. **T⊠ET0530AORD/01MAR—0130PLAX/01MAR**

T⊠MI∧KM∧<Miles> Convert miles to kilometers. For other conversions, see **N*METRIC**. **T⊠MI∧KM∧420** yields **768**

Other Miscellaneous Stuff

N*/<City 3–Letter Code> City sightseeing info. **N*/DCA**

N*<City Code>FON AA airport phone numbers **N*ATLFON**

N*DIAL Area Codes

N*GLOBE∧P<Page Number> Returns country information. Pages 1-16 were available at last update. **N*GLOBE∧P12**

N*PS∧INDEX Admirals Club index of star files

N*INTERNATIONAL International ticketing information for agents

Non-Revenue Related STAR Records

F*PSM/OA/JUMPSEAT Reciprocal jump seat information concerning other company's pilots in AA jump seats. Use **D6** in place of OA to show list of approved carriers. **F*PSM/D6**

N*ACS∧NONREV Automated Check-In System (ACS) non-rev-related code information.

N*IM∧OUTTA∧HERE Non-Revenue index of helpful RES Stars

N*JUMP∧SEAT Jump Seat booking procedure

N*NONRES Non-Revenue AVRS - How To Use

N*TVLDISCOUNTS Worldwide discount fares on AA & others

N*TICKETLESS∧Q∧AND∧A Self Explanatory!!

N*ID90 Non-Revenue Travel Other Airlines, ID90

N*CARS Rental car Information

N*TVLNDX AA Employee Travel Program Index

Other Helpful STAR Records

N*DD<State Abbreviation><1st Letter of City> Postal zip codes and cargo price zones for many AA cities. Example is for Peoria, IL **N*DDILP**

N*GLOBE Geographical data by country

N*MARKET∧CHANGES AA's plans for new & discontinued service, both domestic and international

N*MONEY currency conversion

N*MOONS Full Moon Calendar

N*SKI∧TEAM American Airlines Ski Team

Index Listings of RES Codes and Information

F*SAI Sabre-assisted training table of contents.
N*<Station>NDX Index of station-related Stars **N*ORDNDX**
N*SABCOD General Index for Sabre formats and codes. Includes DECS and RES.
N*SABRE General Sabre use information, with sample formats.
N*SYSHOT System Hot news for agents , as well as many new computer codes (especially RES).

FOCUS System

To access sign in to the RES mode, type **FOCUS** ENTER. The response is the current FOCUS index. Following are examples from that index. The index changes often, so these item numbers may be wrong. When the sample listing was pulled up, there were 58 listings.

To access a selection in which you are interested, simply type **F*<Line Number>** Example: **F*17**

Then, follow instructions on the bottom of each STAR Record. Much of this information is being gradually transitioned to web access, so much of the utility of this system is diminished.

To access a known **FOCUS** topic directly from anywhere in RES, simply use the **F*<Code>** entry, i.e., **F*ACS** or **F*PSM**.

```
---------------- AUTOMATED REFERENCE SYSTEM ----------------
   1. PSM - ATO/CTO PASSENGER SERVICE MANUAL -POLICY/PROCEDUR
   2. LCM - LINE CARGO MANUAL
   3. CSM - CABIN SERVICE MANUAL
   4. TSM - TERMINAL SERVICES MANUAL
              MULTI-HOST REF
  52.                         ERIAL SAFETY
  53. HAZ - ENVIRONMENTAL REFERENCE MANUAL
  54. DLI - AMERICAN AIRLINES DIVERSITY LIBRARY INDEX
  55. SCR - AIRPORT SECURITY MANUAL
  56. ONE - ONEWORLD ALLIANCE MANUAL
  57. AEA - AMERICAN EAGLE TRAINING
  58. AWD - AMERICAN AIRLINES AADVANTAGE AWARD SEARCH
                        END OF LIST
```

Appendix 1: DECS HIDIR or "DF*" Hot Path Entries

This listing includes some of the most commonly used HIDIR hotpaths. Flight crews access this information through HIDIR menus or hotpaths below. Other employee groups access the same information substituting **DF*** for **DIR** in each hotpath code listing.

30 & 7 Waiver Information **DIR/FA/LGL/30**
Add & Removal codes for HI1s, Pilots: **DIR/HELP/CP/CODE**
  Add codes, Flight Attendants: **DIR/FA/ADD**
  Removal codes, Flight Attendants: **DIR/FA/CODE**
AVRS Numbers & Instructions **DIR/CREW/AVRS**
Bid vacancy awards for pilots **DIR/FMFC/VNCY**
Bidding—monthly lines (not PBS) Pilots: **DIR/HELP/CP/BID**
or Flight Attendants: **DIR/FA/BID**
Crew Schedule, Crew Planning, & Crew Resource phone numbers **DIR/CREW/800/CP**
Explanation Of HI1 Addition, Removal Codes **DIR/FA/CODE**
First class seat maps--preference forms **DIR//FA/HELP/FORM**
Flight Attendant information menu **DIR/SVC**
Flight Plan release & weather entries **DIR/HELP/CP/DECS/FLT**
Flight Plan-Related Computer Entries **DIR/FLT/RLS**
HI Entries—complete listing **DIR/HELP/CP/HI–** *or* **DIR/FA/HELP/HI–**
HI Entries—most common **DIR/HELP/CP/HI** *or* **DIR/FA/HELP/HI**
HIDIR Master Index **DIR/HELP/CP/NDX**
HISEND for F/As **DIR/FA/SEND/SEND**
Hotel data for FA variable manning positions **DIR/HTL/VMC/ALL**
Hotel formats & examples. **DIR/HTL/HELP**
Hotels–Regular layover hotel, pickup & station information. Example is **Q**uito, Ecuador station code **UIO.** (Format applies to all hotel entries below.) **DIR/HTL/<1st Letter of City>/<Station>** *Example:* **DIR/HTL/Q/UIO**
Jump Seat Information. (Reciprocal, pilots) Information formerly in HIDIR, now online at www.aapilots.com ***<Resources> <Tools>***
Pay Claim Information: HICLAIM System Instructions; under-staffing, ground/hold times., etc. **DIR/FA/HELP/HELP**
Phone Numbers–Crew 800 number menu overview **DIR/CREW/800/CP** *or* **DIR/FA/VIP/CREW**
Printer Operation information **DIR/HELP/CP/PTR** *or* **DIR/FA/HELP/PTR**
PVD Request procedures **DIR/HELP/CP/PVD** *or* **DIR/FA/VC/PVD**
RES Entries **DIR/HELP/CP/RES**
RES Sign-in **DIR/HELP/CP/RES/SI**

RES Stars—Index to helpful Stars **DIR/HELP/CP/RES/STAR**
Revenue Deposit System - HIDEP **DIR/FA/HELP/DEP**
Revised TDY Procedures **DIR/PLAN/CPLA/TDY**
Send Addresses for use with **HI0** symbolic address messages
DIR/CREW/SEND/SCP/<Station>
Example: **DIR/CREW/SEND/SCP/DFW**
Trip Trade & Bid Services licensed to serve AA crews **DIR/BTRP**
Trip Trade Procedures **DIR/HELP/CP/TT** *or* **DIR/FA/TT**
Trip Trade, Optional Exchange Procedures **DIR/FA/TT**
Weather entry coding formats
DIR/FLT/WEA

Appendix 2: RES Star Files

This listing includes only the most commonly needed STAR records & files.

Airport Phone Numbers for airports served by American Airlines
N*<City 3-Letter Code>FON *Example:* **N*DFWFON**
Airline Reservation Phone Numbers **N*AIR∧PHONE**
Airline discounts **N*TVLDISCOUNTS**
Airport Terminal Maps for selected major hub airports
N*<City 3-Letter Code>MAP *Example:* **N*ORDMAP**
American Airlines Ski Team **N*SKI∧TEAM**
Automated Check-In System (ACS) non-rev-related code information. **N*ACS∧NONREV**
Car Rental Information **N*CARS**
Fare calculation information **N*FARES**
FedEx shipping discounts for AA employees **N*TVLFEDEP**
Frequently used information for station **N*<Station>NDX**
Example: **N*ORDNDX**
Full Moon Calendar **N*MOONS**
General index for DECS and RES formats and codes **N*SABCOD**
Geographical Data By Country **N*GLOBE**
Hotel 800 Numbers **F*PSM/HOTEL**
Hours and miscellaneous details for specified airport
N*<City 3-Letter Code>HRS *Example:* **N*ATLHRS**
ID 90 Travel on other airlines **N*ID90**
Index to corporate Central Division star records **N*INDEX**
International travel document requireements **N*DOCUMENTS**
Non-Revenue Travel On American Airlines **N*NONREV**
Passenger Services - Hot Information
N*SYSHOT<Month MMM> **N*SYSHOTDEC**
State Department (US) travel advisories **N*/ADVISORY∧INDEX**
TPS Codes and Entry Formats **N*TPSAA**
Travel Program Index for AA employees **N*TVLNDX**
Weather Codes for SLS DECS Entries **N*WEATHER**
Wind chill factor chart **N*WIND∧CHILL**
ZED Fare information
N*TVLZEDSC

Appendix 3: Web Pages

This appendix contains only a few of the thousands of airline-related web pages. All web pages below worked when checked, and in the case of companies, they represent companies with whom the author has had positive business dealings.

Airline-Related Web Pages

Allied Pilots Association	www.alliedpilots.org
American Airlines Pilots' Website	www.aapilots.com
American Airlines	www.aa.com
American Airlines Jet Net & E-Pays	www.jetnet.aa.com
Association of Professional Flight Attendants	www.apfa.org
Expedia travel home page	www.expedia.com
Employment verification	www.theworknumber.com
Orbitz travel page	www.orbitz.com
Travelocity travel information	www.travelocity.com

Computer-Related Web Pages

Airline Bidding Solutions (BidPro & FosPro)	www.bidpro.com
BSecure Online Filter	www.bsecure.com
CyberSitter (Internet parental control)	www.solidoak.com
McAfee Corporation	www.mcafee.com
Norton AntiVirus	www.symantec.com
Sabre Group, The	www.sabre.com

Retail Web Sites

Crew Outfitters/Flight Academy Gift Shop	www.crewoutfitters.com
Outer Marker Crew Shop	www.outermarker.com

Aircraft, Military, and General Interest

Airliner Pictures	www.airliners.net
Boeing Corporation	www.boeing.com
Commemorative Air Force	www.commemorativeairforce.org
September 11th Memorial Sites	www.911memorial.org
US Air Force	www.af.mil
US Army	www.army.mil
US Coast Guard	www.uscg.mil
US Marine Corps	www.usmc.mil
US Navy	www.navy.mil

Appendix 4: Key Phone Numbers

Note: *These phone numbers have not been validated for this printing. Please send corrections if you discover them!*

Emergency Phone Numbers and Contacts

Crew bases—For emergency contact numbers, updated daily, see **RF8111 DUTY**

Base	Phone
BOS - Boston	**617-634-5500**
ORD - Chicago	**773-686-4340**
DFW - Dallas/Fort Worth	**972-425-5151**
LAX - Los Angeles	**310-646-2570**
MIA - Miami	**305-526-1230**
LGA - New York - LGA	**718-476-4269**
SFO - San Francisco	**650-877-6094**
STL / SLT - St. Louis	**314-429-9862**
DCA - Washington	**703- 892-7870**

Emergency Numbers

- Crew Scheduling Manager on Duty **817-967-7848**
- Emergency Number **817-967-7800**

Crew Scheduling, Tracking, etc. .... **800-VIP-CREW** *or* **800-847-2739**

- DFW Area **817-956-2739**

Flight Assist Managers	Cell/Pager	Phone
Scott Hansen	**817-874-9160**	**817-967-5291**
Scott.Hansen@aa.com		
Renee Hair	**877-503-3043**	**817-931-9441**
Renee.Hair@aa.com		8777832158@skytel.com
Dena Payne	**866-492-1733**	**817-967-5486**
Dena.Payne@aa.com		86674921733@skytel.com

Systems Operations Control (SOC)

- Manager on Duty **817-967-7100**
- Flight Duty OfficerContact Base Chief Pilot (See above)
  - After Hours **817-967-7050**
  - Duty Chief Information .... **RF8111^DUTY**

Other Contacts

- Allied Pilots' Association (APA) **800-323-1470**
- Assoc. of Prof. Flight Attendants (APFA) **800-395-2732**
- Employment verification **800-367-5690**

Index

Notes: CP –Cockpit Crewmembers FA –Flight Attendants

IND

D

E

F

G

H

I

P

Q

R

IND

U

V

W

Z

Acknowledgments

Cover cartoon by
Deryl Skelton

Special thanks for editorial assistance during past working association with
Captain Chuck Griffin

Book layout, printing and production by

Pilot Study Guides, LLC

Notes

Notes

Titles Currently Available
by Rick Townsend

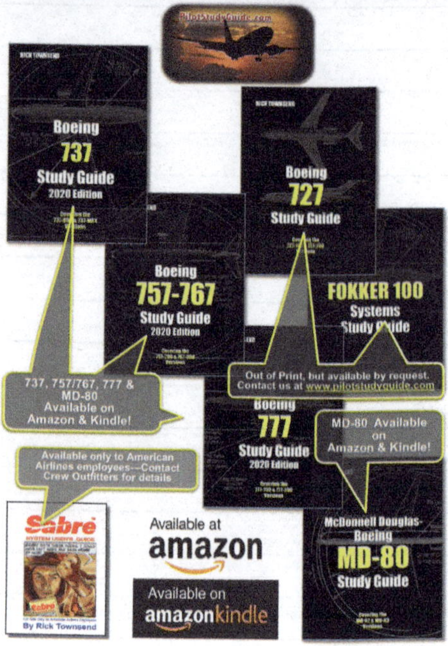

Boeing 777 and 737 Study Guides are available at Crew Outfitters locations at the Flight Academy Gift Shop, or at DFW Airport Terminal C Operations and may be purchased online through **www.crewoutfitters.com**

To order by phone, call **800-874-1204**

For information on electronic study guide releases, go to
www.PilotStudyGuide.com

Snowball Express

GARY SINISE FOUNDATION
SNOWBALL EXPRESS

Serving the children of our fallen military heroes

Snowball Express Could Use Your Help!

OFFICIAL AIRLINE PARTNER American Airlines

The Gary Sinise Foundation's Snowball Express honors America's fallen military service members who have made the ultimate sacrifice since 9/11 by:

1. **Humbly serving the families they left behind**
2. **Championing their children's future success by creating opportunities for joy, friendship, and communal healing**
3. **Connecting these families to one another.**

Since 2006, the mission of Snowball Express has been a simple, yet profoundly important one: Providing hope and new happy memories to the children of military fallen heroes who have died while on active duty since 9/11. In December each year we bring children together from all over the world for a four-day experience filled with fun activities, like sporting events, dances, amusement parks and more.

Nationally, Snowball Express provides comprehensive support programs for fallen families that are focused on transition and connections to community resources, healing and wellness, peer engagement, education and personal/professional development programs.

www.snowballexpress.org

Kenya Kids Can!

Feeding and teaching world changers of tomorrow

Kenya Kids Can is a ministry in the Rift Valley, Kenya. We feed students and construct solar powered computer centers to improve education and bring hope to needy students. Please browse the website to learn about what you can do to truly change lives.

www.kenyakidscan.org

A portion of the proceeds from this book supports this worthy cause. Please consider getting involved and helping as well!

Made in the USA
Monee, IL
03 November 2026

67375829R00046

Notes and Phrases

DRUG ADMINISTRATION

Capsule(s) - Kapsil
Pill(s) - grenn, comprime (Fr.), medikaman
Drop(s) - gout
Dropper - kontgout
Tablespoon(s)- gwo kiye
Teaspoon(s) - ti kiye

Daily (QD) - en fwa chak jou
Twice per day (BID) - de fwa chak jou
Three times per day (TID) - twa fwa chak jou
Four times per day (QID) - kat fwa chak jou
Every ..... hrs. - Chak ..... e

NUMBERS

1/4 - un kar
1/3 - un twazyem
1/2 - mwatiye

1 - en	11 - onz	21 - venteyen
2 - de	12 - douz	22 - ventde
3 - twa	13 - trez	30 - trant
4 - kat	14 - katoz	40 - karant
5 - senk	15 - kenz	50 - senkant
6 - sis	16 - sez	60 - swasant
7 - set	17 - diset	70 - swasandis
8 - uit	18 - dizuit	80 - katreven
9 - nef	19 - diznef	90 - katrevendis
10 - dis	20 - ven	100 - san
1000 - mil	million - milion	